12
Stupid Things
That Mess Up Recovery

Avoiding Relapse
through Self-Awareness
and Right Action

ALLEN BERGER, PH.D.

Hazelden
Publishing

Hazelden Publishing
Center City, Minnesota 55012
hazelden.org/bookstore

Library of Congress Cataloging-in-Publication Data
Berger, Allen, 1952–

   12 stupid things that mess up recovery : avoiding relapse through self-awareness and right action / Allen Berger.

      p.   cm.
   Includes bibliographical references.
   ISBN-13: 978-1-59285-486-8 (softcover)

   1. Addicts—Rehabilitation.   2. Self-help techniques.   3. Substance abuse—Treatment.   I. Title.   II. Title: Twelve stupid things that mess up recovery.
   HV4998.B47 2008
   616.86'03—dc22

                                                    2007051075

Editor's note
The names, details, and circumstances may have been changed to protect the privacy of those mentioned in this publication.

   This publication is not intended as a substitute for the advice of health care professionals.

   Alcoholics Anonymous, AA, the Big Book, and the *Grapevine* are registered trademarks of Alcoholics Anonymous World Services, Inc.

16 15   7 8 9

Cover design by David Spohn
Interior design and typesetting by BookMobile

Dedication

This book is dedicated to all of the men and women who have shared their personal journeys with me during the past thirty-six years. God bless you all! I also dedicate this work to my children, Danielle and Nicolas, who continue to inspire me to be the best father and person I can be. I love you both very much.

12 Stupid Things
That Mess Up Recovery

Contents

Acknowledgments

I want to acknowledge and thank several people. First and foremost, I thank Nick Motu for encouraging me to submit this manuscript to Hazelden. I recognize my editors Karen Chernyaev and Kate Kjorlien for their outstanding suggestions and insights that improved this manuscript. I thank Tom, my sponsor, for his unfailing support and wisdom. I recognize Herb Kaighan and Lauren Dibbs for their feedback on and contributions to the original manuscript. And last, but not least, I acknowledge my friends and family for their ongoing support and encouragement.

Introduction

I believe that if we are truly to recover from the disease of addiction, we must grow up—emotionally. True recovery is the product of humility that emerges from living and practicing a conscious and spiritual life. In order to attain humility, we must be honest with ourselves. This necessarily includes looking at the stupid things we do, today, in our recovery. I use the term *stupid* to indicate the things we do that are self-destructive and not in our best interest.

Before we move on to a discussion about how to identify the underlying causes of self-destructive behavior, I want to share how I selected the twelve issues that I discuss in this book. There must be at least a million stupid things that we can do to mess up recovery—all of them self-destructive. A book cataloging all of these would be unwieldy. I wanted to narrow down the list to a more manageable size so I used the following criteria for my selection. I chose what I considered to be the most commonly confronted and critical issues during the early stages of recovery. I define *early recovery* as the first two years of recovery. The main issues that we confront during this time include breaking the bonds of addiction, establishing a spiritual foundation for our recovery, learning effective tools to deal with ourselves and our relationships, and dealing with the wreckage of our past.

Few of us will relate to all of these issues, but the general themes should be familiar. So without further ado, here are my top twelve nominations for stupid things we do to mess up our recovery:

1. Believing addiction to one substance is the only problem
2. Believing sobriety will fix everything
3. Pursuing recovery with less energy than pursuing addiction
4. Being selectively honest
5. Feeling special and unique
6. Not making amends
7. Using the program to try to become perfect
8. Confusing self-concern with selfishness
9. Playing futile self-improvement games
10. Not getting help for relationship troubles
11. Believing that life should be easy
12. Using the program to handle everything

These twelve things are tried-and-true ways of messing up recovery. In the following chapters, I will elaborate on each of them. Please try and keep an open mind as you read this book. It has been my experience that those who do best in recovery are those who are honest with themselves, open to new ideas and experiences, and willing to take direction.

There's one more thing I want to talk about before we move ahead to the task at hand. As you read about each of these twelve stupid things, please ask yourself, *What would cause me to think in this particular way or behave in this particular manner?* The rest of this introduction presents a series of questions to help you become aware of the causes of self-destructive behaviors. The more we become aware of the underlying cause of a particular belief or behavior, the less it controls our life: *awareness of what we are doing to ourselves—awareness of how we sabotage ourselves—starts the process of change.*

Identifying the Causes of Self-Destructive Behaviors

Psychologists and philosophers throughout modern history have tried to understand why we human beings are so self-destructive. Their discussions have ranged from speculating that a death instinct exists deep within our psyches to believing that personality type, childhood trauma, low self-esteem, or an undercurrent of self-hatred are the culprits behind self-destructive acts.

I believe there are four possibilities to consider when assessing the causes of self-destructive behavior. They are numbered because it is important to consider them in order. I recommend starting with number one and working down the list, until the best fit is discovered:

1. our addiction, or our disease
2. ignorance
3. unreasonable expectations and emotional dependency
4. self-erasure and self-hate

Remember to consider each possibility in sequence. When we identify what motivates or causes our stupid behavior, we begin the process of change. *Awareness starts the process of change.*

Is Our Disease the Culprit?

The first and most important thing to consider when looking for the cause of self-destructive behavior is whether our disease is lurking in the shadows. Let me explain my particular view of addiction, which should help explain why I see this as the most crucial issue to rule out.

Research supported by the National Institute on Drug Abuse (NIDA) has demonstrated that the addict's brain changes once addiction has been established. In one study, researchers assembled two groups of people: one group with a history of cocaine use who were in recovery and one group with no history of drug abuse. Each subject was given a PET scan that generates a computer image of the areas of the brain that are absorbing glucose, which reflects which areas of the brain are active.

In the first phase of the study, researchers showed the subjects a video of a hummingbird. In the next phase, they showed the subjects a video of drug-related paraphernalia. In both phases, researchers performed brain scans and collected images. The results revealed that a part of the brain called the amygdala lit up when the recovering drug addicts watched the drug-related video but was inactive when they watched the other video. The amygdala is part of the reward center of the brain. The amygdala did not light up when subjects who never used cocaine observed the drug-related video. This study and numerous others clearly demonstrate that the addict's brain is different from the normal person's brain. Once the brain has been changed by addiction, it is changed forever.

This research supports what has been said for many years in the substance-abuse field: addiction is like a tiger lying in wait for its prey. Unfortunately, *we* are the prey! The tiger is extremely patient as it waits for the optimal moment to pounce on its unsuspecting victim. It is well camouflaged with denial, minimization, rationalization, and other psychological defenses, so it is hard to distinguish the menace from its surroundings. It is extremely powerful and can kill or maim with its first strike, especially when the addiction is to methamphetamine or cocaine. Its stealth makes it hard to identify as it is sneaking up and preparing to attack. Addiction is cunning and baffling. Many times its victims do not know they are being stalked until it is too late.

What makes matters even worse is that our opponent—our addiction—knows everything about us. It is a part of us; it has all the intelligence, capabilities, insights, and knowledge that we possess. It's like we are in a life-and-death struggle against a clone. Our disease anticipates our every move. It understands our strategies. It knows our strengths and weaknesses.

From this discussion, we can see why recovery is so difficult and elusive, and why so many people struggle to get well. I have seen figures that indicate that 80 percent of newcomers relapse in their first year.

It is imperative to begin recovery with *surrender.* We cannot defeat addiction in the traditional sense. The solution begins with a paradox: victory is achieved through surrender, not in battle.

When we totally and unconditionally surrender, which means that we accept our total and complete powerlessness over our addiction, we begin to build a solid foundation for recovery. If we surrender, our disease loses its control over our life. It doesn't disappear. It doesn't go away. It never goes away! It merely recedes into the background. Yet it's always there, like that tiger, waiting for when we have a lapse in our spiritual program, when we are feeling down and out because we have just gotten into a bitter argument with our spouse, or when we have received a special recognition at work and feel that we deserve to celebrate. It will act on any opportunity to regain control of our life. The stronger our recovery, the more subtle and insidious are addiction's efforts to sabotage us. Beware!

Now let's use this discussion of addiction to understand self-destructive behavior. The first thing to consider is whether our disease is once again trying to establish a foothold in our life. It may be setting us up in order to take charge and again run the show. Remember, it is always looking for that opportunity to convince us to return to drinking or using other drugs.

Often a person enters treatment and looks for all the ways that his using isn't as bad as those around him. He argues, "I wasn't that out of control and didn't lose my job. My spouse hasn't left. I only had one DUI. I never experienced a blackout. I didn't drink in the morning. I never hid the bottles." The list can go on and on and on. Before long, he has convinced himself that he can return to drinking; he will just need to control it better this time around. This is an example of a person who has not truly surrendered.

The disease is capable of convincing us to go ahead and drink again, because this time it will be different. "You are not a real alcoholic!" is what it is covertly saying. The addicted part of us will insist on this position, despite overwhelming evidence to the contrary. Why? Because the disease will selectively ignore information that validates our powerlessness. This filtering is called *selective inattention.* The information that indicates we are an alcoholic and unable to control our drinking is ignored.

Watching out for how the beast may be sabotaging our recovery is crucial. So watch and listen. It will be our own life that we save if we keep a constant vigil.

Is Ignorance Our Problem?

If we have not found evidence that we are being ambushed by our disease, then we need to consider whether our self-destructive behavior may be a result of our *ignorance.* Many of us need to look no further than this to understand why we behave the way we do. *We can only do what we have been taught to do.* We don't know what we don't know. We can't act on what we don't know.

Let's face a difficult and painful truth: most of us don't know how to live an authentic, effective, healthy, and fulfilling life. This fact is obvious, but we resist seeing it and facing it. We don't want to see our limitations. We don't want to face our shortcomings because that means we'll have to do something about them. We'll have to work at getting and learning new information. We'll have to ask for help. Men and women are equally inept when it comes to knowing how to live a balanced and satisfying life. Our unreasonable expectations create a false pride that prohibits us from letting others know that we do not have the answers—that we need help. Some of us try to become needless or wantless. When our false pride is in charge, ignorance becomes something of which to be ashamed. Being ignorant doesn't fit with our self-image, so we disown it. We become more concerned with "saving face rather than saving our behinds."

A couple once came to my office to seek counseling for a serious marital problem that was taking them to the brink of divorce. As Mark saw it, Sheila was the problem because she had reneged on an agreement (made before they were married) that she would stay at home and care for their future children. In the agreement, Sheila would resign from her job and make the family her new job. Mark was a very successful businessman, and Sheila did not have to work for them to enjoy a very high standard of living. After having a daughter, Sheila resigned from her job and in a short time became very unhappy. She loved raising their daughter but did not feel complete without her work. She wanted to do both and decided to return to work as a consultant. This infuriated Mark; he felt betrayed and abandoned. The tension in their marriage escalated, and they would have long unproductive talks during which Mark would berate and criticize Sheila. She emotionally withdrew, building walls to protect herself. Mark's worst fear (Sheila emotionally abandoning him) was realized, but he didn't understand that he had contributed to the problem. He was so focused on her, on blaming her for his pain, that he couldn't see his part: by blaming her, he alienated her. This was his blind spot. He did not understand that whenever there is a problem in a relationship, both parties contribute to the difficulty. As a child, Mark grew up with the family myth that when there is a relationship problem, there is one person to blame for it. Once he understood that this was just a myth he was raised to believe, he began to have successful experiences in relating to his wife. Because of this shift in his perspective, the marriage miraculously turned around. They fell in love all over again, and they have learned an important life lesson together.

So poke around in this area and see if it is relevant before considering the next possibility. Some of us find that our ignorance and the false pride that protects it are two of the culprits underlying our self-defeating behaviors.

Are We Emotionally Dependent and Trying to Live Up to Unreasonable Expectations?

The third consideration is emotional dependency and the unreasonable expectations it breeds. In a letter to a dear friend who was suffering from depression, Bill Wilson, co-founder of Alcoholics Anonymous (AA), shared what he had discovered as a result of his battle with depression and his search for a cure. The letter, reprinted in 1958 as an article in the *Grapevine,* was titled "The Next Frontier: Emotional Sobriety." Bill argued that once we move beyond the actual mental obsession and physical craving for alcohol, the next issue we face becomes maintaining emotional balance in our life. Bill realized that the cause of his underlying emotional instability was an "absolute dependence—on people or circumstances to supply me with prestige, security, and the like." Bill believed, as I do, that until we break this absolute dependence on people, places, and things, we will not be able to find real peace of mind. This idea wasn't new. It had been discussed in the field of psychology too. Psychotherapists referred to Bill's "absolute dependency" as emotional dependency.

Most alcoholics or addicts think of themselves as highly sensitive people because of how easily their feelings are hurt in their relationships. The truth is that it is not a high sensitivity that causes this response. When we rely on another person for validation, we become highly reactive to however he or she acts or to whatever he or she thinks. Emotional dependency makes us highly reactive in our relationships because other people become too important. The more important a person is, the more likely our emotional dependency will undermine the relationship. If we suffer from emotional dependency, we allow another person to define our reality.

For example, a client of mine was upset because her husband did not enjoy what she had cooked for dinner. She was proud of the effort she extended to produce their meal. He didn't like the new dish, and she was devastated. She felt great about what she had done until his reaction. She tried something new, took a risk, but because he didn't like it, she was unable to continue to pat herself on the back for her effort. She let him define her reality. When we are emotionally dependent, we are looking for personal validation from others. We develop what David Schnarch, Ph.D., referred to as a "reflected self-image." Our self-image is determined by how others behave toward us.

Our emotional dependency may also manifest in our relationships as demands on how others should behave toward us. This is to ensure that we won't feel insecure or anxious. In the previous example, the woman's implicit demand on the relationship was that "He must like everything I do!" Quite a tall order, isn't it? Emotional dependency creates demands and brings about unrealistic expectations in our relationships.

Whether we realize it or not, we are all emotionally dependent to some degree—most of the time we don't realize it until we have been hit over the head with a two-by-four. Living with unreasonable expectations is like trying to fit the proverbial square peg into the round hole. The result is complete and utter frustration. But does that stop us? Hell no! We try harder! We pick up a bigger hammer and hit that stubborn square peg with even greater force, oftentimes shattering it to pieces. And when we stand back and analyze our failed efforts, we blame it on the square peg: "If only that person would just _____, we could have a wonderful relationship."

When our expectations go unchallenged or when we expect others to live up to our expectations, we set ourselves up for trouble and we set our partner up for failure. Unreasonable expectations are typically rationalized, which disguises their true and unreasonable nature. Once we have deceived ourselves into believing our behavior is justified, we have a license to act in destructive and tyrannical ways. Tyrannical behavior destroys love and alienates those close to us. We rarely realize that beneath our impossible set of demands on others lies emotional dependency. Other people *must* treat us a certain way, or it indicates to us that we aren't all right. Remember the idea of reflected self-image? If "they" do not comply with our unreasonable demands, it becomes personal. It means that they do not love us and that we are undesirable, unlovable, inadequate.

So we need to critically question our expectations. If we are honest with ourselves, we will find a script in our head about how things are supposed to be. When people don't live up to our expectations, we try to manipulate them or control the situation to get them to behave the way we want them to. If they don't, we become demanding and resentful. If this doesn't work, we may fall into a depression or have panic attacks. I heard a great line in a meeting once: "expectations are premeditated resentments." So if recovery isn't all that it is promised to be, it's quite possible that emotional dependency is limiting it.

Are Self-Erasure and Self-Hate Causing Our Problems?

The final area to explore concerns two different issues: self-erasing and self-hate. While these two behaviors manifest themselves differently, they share a similar core dynamic: the alienation or rejection of the true self.

Self-erasing is a term that was coined by Theodore Isaac Rubin, M.D. Self-erasing is seeking emotional security by not being present in our life. This way of living makes no waves and discourages others from taking notice. Tiptoeing through life becomes natural because our goal is to avoid conflict and rejection. We deny and repress our needs. We try to be invisible. We dread expressing our opinion, and we go to great lengths to avoid taking a stand. We will not assert our needs or desires. It is almost as if we are saying, "Please don't notice me. I don't want to be seen." This is a complete rejection of ourselves—a total abandonment of self because of fear.

Once again, the underlying problem is emotional dependency. When we function from other-validated self-esteem, everyone's reactions have too much weight. Their reactions are too important. They have the power to make us feel good or bad. This leads to an avoidance of both authenticity and intimacy. If we are self-erasing, then we are sabotaging our life. Any life based on a rejection of or alienation from self is doomed to failure.

If we are self-erasing, we are selling ourselves short. We are all much more capable and much less fragile than we believe. Most of us can learn how to face and resolve conflicts.

Self-hate is the next culprit to consider. This is one of the most frequently undiagnosed causes of self-destructive behavior. Self-hate begins when we don't live up to being the person we think we should be. We all develop an idealized image of who we are supposed to be. We rarely question this standard; we accept it wholeheartedly and uncritically. As this idealized image is established, we also develop a pride system that demands we live up to these standards. When we don't live up to our "shoulds," we despise ourselves. We hate ourselves for being less than what we "should" be.

Self-hate is deeply rooted in and continuously influenced by our behavior, even though we may not be aware of it. *I am convinced that self-hate is one of the primary causes of relapse.* A person simply does not feel worthy of recovery, worthy of getting better, worthy of receiving help, worthy of joy, happiness, success, freedom, and love. This leads to many direct and indirect expressions of self-hate. Undermining our recovery is one of the ways that self-hate can manifest itself in our life. To look into this subject in greater detail, please get a copy of Theodore Isaac Rubin's book *Compassion and Self-Hate: An Alternative to Despair.*

I believe each and every one of us in recovery struggles with each of these issues to some degree. We now have four different levels of analysis to assess and understand self-destructive behavior. We can keep these four sources of self-destructive behavior in mind when reading the rest of this book. Each source provides us with clues and helps us deal with self-destructive behavior so that we can ultimately realize the promises of recovery. The final chapter of this book presents several suggestions for how to address these issues.

Stupid Thing 1
Believing Addiction to One Substance Is the Only Problem

Our best chance for recovery lies in total abstinence from all mind-altering drugs.

It is quite common for men and women who are beginning recovery to minimize the extent and severity of their problem. When I was working as a clinical supervisor in an inpatient chemical dependency treatment program, patients would often try to convince me that they really didn't have a problem with the other drugs they were using; it was just the alcohol. Hearing these beliefs over and over again raised the following question: Why would someone trying to get help for a drinking problem, for example, ignore or minimize the fact that smoking marijuana is also part of the problem?

The answer was simple: The person is trying to deceive himself into thinking that he is normal and can control his behavior. He desperately wants to believe that he can still get high, even though he might have to stop drinking. He does not want to see the truth: he is powerless over all mind-altering drugs. This kind of self-deception is prevalent in many shapes and forms. Alcoholics may fool themselves into thinking that they can no longer drink whiskey but can have a beer every now and again. There is a growing problem in AA of members saying they are "sober" while still occasionally smoking marijuana.

The mind is remarkable in how it creates self-deception. We can keep ourselves from seeing the truth about ourselves and our behavior in many different ways. The technical term for this type of mental defense mechanism is *compartmentalization*. When we compartmentalize a problem, we keep it isolated, or separated, from other relevant issues. In this instance, we compartmentalize our alcohol or drug abuse. We keep an ace up our sleeve in case the going gets tough. Drinking or using is still an option. When we keep this kind of a secret, we are sabotaging our recovery. What we need to do is to share this secret—tell the truth. When we do, we give ourselves a chance to connect the dots.

Here's an example from my own personal recovery. I returned to the United States from Vietnam in 1971 with a serious drug problem, as did thousands of other veterans. At that time, I mistakenly believed that drugs other than alcohol were my problem. I didn't even think of alcohol as a drug, which it is. I was about three weeks into my recovery when I hitchhiked from the west side of Oahu to Honolulu to meet with Tom, my sponsor, and then go to an AA meeting. A local man picked me up in his Toyota Corolla. He had a six-pack of beer in his front seat. He offered me one of the beers, and without much thought, I thanked him and drank it. When Tom opened his door and greeted me, he looked disturbed because he could smell the alcohol on my breath. He asked me whether I had been drinking. I immediately said I had had a beer and quite naively added that he didn't have to worry because I didn't have a problem with alcohol—just drugs. He looked at me with that look that a sponsor has when he knows you are full of it. He asked me to sit down, said we had a lot to discuss. About three hours later, I realized that alcohol was a drug and that I was deceiving myself. I had an epiphany after Tom invited me to share my history of using alcohol and other drugs. As I told him about my life, he underscored the obvious: before I started using other drugs, I was having serious problems with alcohol. I experienced blackouts, compromised personal values, lived to drink, and drank to live. He helped me connect the dots, and once they were connected, I no longer compartmentalized my use of alcohol.

The truth is that our best chance for recovery lies in total abstinence. Here are five reasons why:

1. Use of any drugs increases the likelihood of using our drug of choice.
2. Cross-addiction is likely to occur.
3. We do not learn from our experiences while we are using.
4. Complete recovery requires total abstinence.
5. Drugs numb or soothe our feelings and therefore interfere with recovery.

Let's explore these in more detail.

Use of Any Drugs Increases the Likelihood of Using Our Drug of Choice

Most chemical dependency counselors warn their clients that using other drugs lowers their resistance to using their drug of choice. For example, studies over the years have repeatedly shown that relapses among people treated for cocaine problems occur most frequently when they are under the influence of alcohol. Many recovering alcoholics relapse after receiving medications such as Vicodin, Valium, Xanax, or Klonopin. Recovering alcoholics who smoke marijuana typically return to drinking. Heroin addicts are more likely to go out and try to score after drinking alcohol.

Another important thing to remember is *a drug is a drug.* Therefore, the use of any mind-altering drug for the purpose of getting high is a relapse.

Cross-Addiction Is Likely to Occur

Addicts are vulnerable to switching addictions to another drug. This is called *cross-addiction.* I recently treated a man who proudly declared that he had conquered a heroin problem several years ago, yet he minimized the fact that he was having problems in several areas of his life because of his abuse of methamphetamine. When I confronted him about his cross-addiction, he declared, "I can stop if I really put my mind to it!"

The truth was that he had been trying to stop for several months and couldn't. He wasn't using every day, but when he did use, he could not predict whether he would be able to control how much he was going to use. Many times he promised himself that he was not going to drink or use meth but was unable to honor his intentions. In fact, he broke his promises to himself at least twelve times during six months. Everyone but him could see that *he could not control his use of meth.* He was blind to the reality that he was an addict, which meant he didn't have the ability to regulate his use of drugs—any drugs. Addiction changes the brain, and he had already lost the ability to control his use of drugs.

What happened to this young man is very common in addiction. Vernon Johnson, D.D., founder of the Johnson Institute, described this thought process as a *sincere delusion.* We truly believe the promises we make. We're so sincere when we make a commitment that we would pass a lie detector test, but the truth is that we are out of touch with reality. The reality that is so difficult for us to accept is that we do not have the ability to control our use of alcohol or other drugs. When we unconditionally accept this reality, we can build a solid foundation for recovery.

We Do Not Learn from Our Experiences While We Are Using

The client whom I discussed earlier was unable to learn from his experience. This is one of the most common personality traits among addicts. While behavioral scientists have been unable to identify a definitive *addictive personality,* one thing is certain: *alcoholics and addicts do not learn from their experience.* There are three reasons for this: *denial, drug-induced brain dysfunction,* and *state-dependent learning.* Denial is psychological, while the other two are neuro-psychological. Let's discuss the psychological process of denial first.

Psychological Processes That Interfere with Learning

Addicts and alcoholics have difficulty learning from experience because they are invested in maintaining the illusion that everything is all right. We truly believe that we control our behavior despite an overwhelming amount of evidence that suggests otherwise. This is, by definition, delusional thinking. A delusion is a belief that is not supported by reality. The belief that we are in control, when in reality we are not, is delusional. This false perception is fostered by denial.

Denial is a defense mechanism. It protects us from the truth, especially when the truth is painful. We do not want to see reality because of what it ultimately means. For us, the truth is that we are not able to drink or use other drugs—we are not who we thought we were. Our self-esteem cannot face this harsh reality, so we alter our reality. We pretend to be something we are not. We cannot accept reality's limitations. Denial needs to be penetrated or shattered before we can truly admit that we are totally powerless over alcohol and other drugs.

Neuropsychological Processes That Interfere with Learning

Another reason alcoholics and addicts have difficulty learning from experience involves the neuropsychology of addiction and how alcohol and other drug use affect learning.

During the past forty years, an extensive body of literature has demonstrated both the short- and long-term effects of heavy drinking on the brain. The most severe result of chronic alcoholism is a disorder called Korsakoff's syndrome, which includes severe memory loss. But this is an extreme. Most alcoholics suffer from mild to moderate, reversible, *drug-induced brain dysfunction,* which affects abstract thinking and the ability to problem solve. When abstract thinking is impaired, learning is impaired. We do not draw the proper conclusions from our experiences. Instead, we make and defend incorrect deductions. When we are faced with how our behavior is altered by our abuse of drugs, we evaluate the information with a malfunctioning organ: our brain. It is like asking a broken computer to tell us that it is broken.

Another important process to consider is *state-dependent learning.* This concept helps explain how drug use affects the ability to mature emotionally. Years ago, researchers demonstrated state-dependent learning with the following experiment. Two groups of rats were taught to run a complex maze. Prior to the training, one group of rats was injected with alcohol. The other group of rats was sober. Both groups learned to run the maze in about the same length of time. Their learning curves were quite similar. The differences between the groups became apparent the following day when they were again placed in the maze to see how much learning they retained.

The group of rats who were sober when they learned to run the maze did fine. They had no difficulty finding the hunk of cheese at the end. The rats who were injected with alcohol before they learned how to run the maze acted as though they had never seen the maze before. What they learned did not transfer to their sober condition.

State-dependent learning explains why many alcoholics and addicts are emotionally arrested at early stages of their development. We have not learned from our experiences. Learning from our life experiences is necessary for the development of emotional maturity.

Denial, drug-induced brain dysfunction, and state-dependent learning explain why it is so difficult for us to be self-aware, see the true extent of our problems, learn from past experiences, and mature emotionally.

Let's now return to a discussion of the fourth factor in the argument for total abstinence in recovery.

Complete Recovery Requires Total Abstinence

The fourth reason for total abstinence is that if we continue to drink or use other drugs, we cannot fully be present and accessible during the process of recovery. Recovery requires total honesty, open-mindedness, and willingness. Using alcohol and other drugs interferes with our ability to be honest with ourselves, to be open-minded regarding our life and how we have managed it, to experiment with new ways of dealing with life, and to discover a spiritual solution to our problems.

In a recent conference on recovery, Garrett O'Connor, M.D., a well-known psychiatric expert on alcoholism and addiction, noted that "Addiction is a medical disease with a spiritual cure." Many mental health professionals have discovered that a spiritual cure is the most effective solution for dealing with an alcohol or drug problem. We cannot discover our spirituality if we are drinking or using.

Many people believe that we discover spirituality through pain. Hurting and suffering can inspire us to muster the courage to look down—way down—into the soul and see what we fear and loathe. We must die before we can be reborn. We must descend before we can ascend.

Our mind is the seat of our perceptions, experiences, memories, decision making, judgment, emotions, and consciousness. If we alter it with drugs, we cannot see the truth about ourselves or feel emotional pain, both of which are necessary to facilitate recovery and live life fully.

So keep the following in mind: *when we are feeling bad in the early stages of recovery, we are doing well.* Early work in recovery requires us to feel worse in order to grow spiritually. We need to go down into our soul and into the darkness before we can ascend on the spiritual path.

Drugs Numb or Soothe Our Feelings and Therefore Interfere with Recovery

The fifth and final reason for total abstinence is related to how alcohol and other drugs soothe or numb our feelings. We have all, at one time or another, wanted to numb our feelings for various reasons.

Our society is pain phobic. We avoid dealing with pain in any way we can. Just watch the television ads during a normal evening of programming to see how many commercials offer us a quick way of escaping discomfort or pain. The message we get throughout our life is that painful feelings are undesirable, unnecessary, and unwelcome. It should be no surprise that most of us will go to great lengths to avoid feeling pain of any kind. We have pursued numbness fearlessly and tenaciously, which has led us right through the gates of addiction and insanity.

Recovery is the antithesis of addiction. Instead of running away from our problems, we face them. Instead of avoiding our feelings, we embrace them. Instead of drowning out the voice of pain, we listen to it. Instead of avoiding ourselves, we confront ourselves. Recovery is the process of recovering our true self and is contingent on becoming honest with ourselves. I wrote a poem that was inspired by a man who was struggling with his pain in my monthly men's group. It's called "A Man Stirs":

A man stirs in his bed.
Are the sheets too silky or soft?
Or are they too cold?
His wife says, "It's all in his head."
I think it is something twitching in his soul.

How will he know?
It is the pain that opens the door.

It is the pain that will make him listen to the voice
    within—he doesn't want to hear.
It is the pain that will make him see the reality—
    he has dared not consider.
It is the pain that will make him experience the
    feelings—he had been reluctant to face.
It is the pain that will help him find the words—
    he has dared not voice.

It is the pain that will open the door to his life,
    but it is only he who can walk through it.

In recovery, we learn that pain can be an ally rather than an enemy. Pain offers important information, if we hold still long enough to listen to it. Our pain can help us learn about our needs—what our working points are—and give us insight into our wounds and personal shortcomings. All grist for the recovery mill.

Holding still and feeling our pain is an important recovery skill, and if experienced in a therapeutic way, it can help us tap inner resources to soothe ourselves and lick our wounds. Total abstinence is necessary to begin true recovery. We sabotage our recovery if we continue to selectively use any mind-altering drugs.*

* The only exception to this rule is psychiatric medication prescribed by a psychiatrist, addictionologist, or physician.

Stupid Thing 2
Believing Sobriety Will Fix Everything

Recovery begins with breaking the bonds of addiction. But this is only the first step on a long journey. Recovery is ultimately about recovering our spiritual, or true, self.

If drinking were our only problem, then once we stopped drinking, all our problems would be solved. Instead, as newly sober people, we discover that there is much more to solving our problems than just putting the cork in the bottle. For example, a man I have been treating for the past several years came to see me shortly after he had completed a month-long treatment program. The program was highly successful in helping him break the bonds of his physical addiction to alcohol. But what he soon discovered was that he was chronically depressed. There were several reasons for his depression, but let's focus on one of them: people were not doing what he thought they should be doing. When they did not meet his demands, he reacted to their behavior by either becoming enraged or depressed. He wanted to direct people to behave the way he wanted them to because he did not know how to deal with disappointment. He placed impossible demands on those he loved. He knew that his expectations were destroying these relationships, but he did not know how to stop. When he could not force others to comply with his demand for perfect security, prestige, or romance, he felt defeated, angry, miserable, and depressed.

While the circumstances may be somewhat different, this scene is quite common and leads to the essence of this chapter, which includes good news and bad news. The good news: if we have broken the bonds of addiction, we are off to a great start. The bad news: our job has only just begun once we have stopped drinking or using. It does not end! Much more than just putting the cork in the bottle needs to be done to ensure full recovery.

Harry Tiebout, M.D., a brilliant psychiatrist who was one of the first professionals to see the value and importance of AA, described alcoholism as "a symptom that has become pathogenic itself." Dr. Tiebout was saying that alcoholism begins as a solution to emotional problems but eventually becomes as much or more of a problem than the original emotional problem. To achieve a full and complete recovery, we must address both sides of the coin: the addiction and the underlying issues.

In a similar vein, Karl Menninger, M.D., used the metaphor of a man jumping off a pier into twenty feet of water because his clothes are on fire to describe the results of turning to addiction as a solution to emotional problems. The man puts out the fire, but he ends up drowning because he jumped.

What these brilliant men were saying is that alcoholics and addicts have emotional problems, and these problems have contributed to their use of alcohol or other drugs. But beware! Don't let this statement mislead you into thinking that all you need to do is to address your emotional problems to recover from this insidious disease. In fact, well-intentioned mental health professionals have tried this approach since the early 1930s, and it has failed miserably.

What these therapists realized was that if we do not deal with the drinking first, then we are not able to deal with any of the other problems. So we should be careful not to let a well-intentioned therapist mislead us into thinking that once we have solved our emotional problems, drinking or using will automatically be curtailed or that we can safely drink or use again.

Our best bet for a complete recovery is to have a two-pronged attack to our problem. We need to deal with both our addiction and the underlying problems. Following is a list of the components for a complete and comprehensive approach to treating addiction:

1. First is the *direct treatment of the symptom* (the alcoholism or other chemical dependency). This phase of treatment deals with breaking the psychological and physiological bonds of addiction.

2. Second is *repairing the deleterious effects of the addiction,* which involves our psychological, physical, emotional, and spiritual health, and the emotional health of our family.

3. Third is the *treatment of the underlying psychological and family issues.* This involves growing up emotionally and learning how to have healthy relationships. This has been defined by Earnie Larsen as *Stage II recovery.*

I hope the question you are now asking yourself is *How do I do all this?* There are many good answers to this question. Thirty years of clinical practice have shown me that the best results are achieved through a combination of rigorously working a Twelve Step program (Alcoholics Anonymous or Narcotics Anonymous) and getting help from an experiential psychotherapist or addictions counselor who fully understands family dynamics and the disease process of addiction.

A Fit Spiritual Condition

For many, remaining clean and sober means developing what page 85 of the Big Book of AA refers to as a "fit spiritual condition." The concept of spirituality is relevant, and for good reason. Discovering and connecting to a spiritual force provides us with the strength and ability to remain clean and sober. This is attained through the development of humility.

The Twelve Steps of AA are designed to connect us with a power greater than ourselves. To find sobriety and stay clean and sober, we have to get out of our own way. We have to learn to be humble. The attainment of humility is accomplished systematically, by working the Twelve Steps in order. In addition to helping us break the bond of addiction—the most immediate concern of addicts—the Twelve Steps also teach us about living life more effectively and harmoniously.

Humility is a prerequisite for spirituality. Humility is experienced by adopting a perspective about life that places "self" within a bigger picture. For the alcoholic or addict, this is quite a shock indeed. We have been so overly concerned with *ourselves* that we act as though we are the center of the universe. We have been obsessed with controlling our drinking or using despite overwhelming evidence that we cannot. *We are not that important and we are not in control,* and we must accept this ego-deflating truth in order to begin recovery.

How do we develop this perspective? Humility starts when we fully surrender to the First Step of the program of AA: "We admitted we were powerless over alcohol—that our lives had become unmanageable." Admitting that we are powerless over alcohol and that our life is unmanageable deflates the almighty ego. We can count on our ego protesting this act of surrender. It will fight this admission with every resource at its disposal. Therefore, our first effort in recovery is to surrender, which begins an ego-deflating campaign. Working the Steps is an excellent way to conduct our campaign.

Humility is just one of the therapeutic effects of working the Steps. There are other therapeutic effects as well, which I have discussed in detail in my pamphlet *The Therapeutic Value of the 12 Steps*. A brief description and summary of the therapeutic value of each Step is presented in the following table.

The Therapeutic Value of the Twelve Steps

Step Number	Text of the Step	Therapeutic Value of the Step
1	We admitted we were powerless over alcohol—that our lives had become unmanageable.	This Step helps us shatter our reliance on a false self.
2	Came to believe that a Power greater than ourselves could restore us to sanity.	Hope is an important ingredient in all forms of healing. In this Step, we are given hope and humbled further because we won't be able to solve our problem on our own.
3	Made a decision to turn our will and our lives over to the care of God *as we understood Him.*	This Step is about commitment. We need to make a commitment to finding a new and more effective way of living.
4	Made a searching and fearless moral inventory of ourselves.	The essence of this Step involves increasing our self-awareness, self-honesty, and insight into our behavior.

Step Number	Text of the Step	Therapeutic Value of the Step
5	Admitted to God, to ourselves, and to another human being the exact nature of our wrongs.	In this Step, we learn the value of self-disclosure, authenticity, and healthy relationships. This Step also continues to dismantle the false self and false pride and helps develop more humility and authenticity.
6	Were entirely ready to have God remove all these defects of character.	In this Step, we experience the pain of what we have done to hurt ourselves and others, and we begin to understand and develop insight into our behavioral patterns and the psychological functions of our character defects.
7	Humbly asked Him to remove our shortcomings.	In this Step, we are learning the importance of being vulnerable and asking for help. This is important in attaining more humility.
8	Made a list of all persons we had harmed, and became willing to make amends to them all.	The lessons taught in Step 8 have to do with the fundamentals of healthy communication: delivering our message to the proper person and being as specific as possible.

Step Number	Text of the Step	Therapeutic Value of the Step
9	Made direct amends to such people wherever possible, except when to do so would injure them or others.	In this Step, we learn to be responsible for our behavior; we learn how to respect others; and we learn that we are as important as others, no more and no less.
10	Continued to take personal inventory and when we were wrong promptly admitted it.	This Step concerns maintaining our humility, being honest with ourselves, and guarding against false pride.
11	Sought through prayer and meditation to improve our conscious contact with God *as we understood Him,* praying only for knowledge of His will for us and the power to carry that out.	Maintenance is not enough. We need to continue to grow or we will regress. This Step is about expanding our consciousness and continuing to seek more knowledge about our new way of life.
12	Having had a spiritual awakening as the result of these steps, we tried to carry this message to alcoholics, and to practice these principles in all our affairs.	In this Step, we develop a new purpose to our life that is not about us. We discover the importance of being of value to others, and we learn that we need to maintain our integrity in all our affairs.

The Steps are a powerful program of change. They evoke a multitude of healing forces that can save our life and open doors we would never have thought possible. But we never know what we are going to find when one of those doors swings open. One epiphany I had in my early recovery was realizing that nothing was as it seemed. For example, I was always afraid that I would discover that I was insane. In recovery, I learned that I was, and in a sense, this was a relief. I didn't fear it anymore. I just accepted myself and got on with establishing a foundation for my recovery. It's almost like I was knocking on the door of insanity all of my life, and when it opened, I realized I was knocking from the inside.

While the Steps offer an incredible formula for change, we have to do the work. *No one will do it for us!* We have to reach down and dig deep and confront ourselves as we have never done before. We will feel worse before we feel better, and we need to give up trying to find an easier, softer way. We must accept that life can be difficult and that most of the time the path of lesser resistance isn't the best one. We need to quit trying to get other people to yield to our demands so that we can feel better about ourselves. Our dependency on other people for our self-esteem is an underlying problem. To change this, we need to learn how to hold on to ourselves and take responsibility for our own feelings. This is the next step in our recovery once we have established a strong foundation for being clean and sober.

Stupid Thing 3
Pursuing Recovery with Less Energy Than Pursuing Addiction

We have to pursue recovery with the same tenacity
and enthusiasm that we had when we were
drinking or using other drugs.

The extremes that an alcoholic or addict will go to in order to use or obtain drugs is remarkable. It indicates the degree of control that the disease has over our life. Here is an example.

I know of a man who would only eat dinner at one particular restaurant. Why was he so loyal to this establishment? The reason for his loyalty had nothing to do with the quality of the food or the wonderful service. Instead, he was motivated by the physical layout of the restaurant and how this created a clandestine opportunity to drink.

Let me describe what this clever alcoholic had figured out about this restaurant. The restroom was located at the other end of the dining room, which meant that he would have to leave the dining section, turn around a corner, and pass in front of the bar before he could access the restroom. His routine was as follows: After being seated with his wife, the server would come and take their order for cocktails. He would order a double scotch and water. Shortly after the server left their table, he would excuse himself to go to the restroom. On his way to the restroom, he would stop at the bar, order a double scotch on the rocks, and drink it rather quickly. After finishing this cocktail, he would proceed to the restroom. After taking care of his business in the restroom, he would sometimes stop at the bar for one more quick drink before returning to his table. By the time he rejoined his wife at their table, the drink he originally ordered was waiting for him.

Unbeknownst to his wife, the man had already consumed two doubles and was on his third. He would repeat this ruse at least once more during the course of the evening. You can imagine that within a couple of hours he would end up highly intoxicated, which would perplex his wife because she only witnessed him having two or three drinks. He would then attribute his state of intoxication to something other than his excessive use of alcohol, and because his wife did not know any better, she would believe him. His ruse worked.

This well-executed plan shows the insidious nature of the alcoholic's thinking. When his wife would suggest another restaurant, he would vehemently object. And we know why.

The power of addiction is evident not only in intricate ruses like the one just described but also in how it can override strong, natural instincts, such as self-preservation. Let me give you two examples.

Meet Catherine. She is a twenty-eight-year-old, single, well-educated woman with a bachelor's degree in economics. She had once been rated one of the top tennis players in Florida, yet her life was a mess for several years because she used crack cocaine.

Catherine's addiction was very powerful. In one of our therapy sessions, she recounted a terrifying example of the force of this juggernaut. About six months prior to reaching out for help, she went to the housing projects in San Pedro, California, to buy some crack cocaine. This area in San Pedro is crawling with drug dealers, prostitutes, and gang members.

It was around midnight when she was driving in this part of town hoping to see her dealer, which she did. He was standing on the usual poorly lit street corner. She pulled up next to him, and as usual, he came over to the car window on the driver's side of the vehicle. This time, however, he convinced her to let him join her in the car so he could show her what he had for sale. After entering the vehicle, he pulled out a gun and forced her to drive to a dark and deserted street. She experienced a horrific sexual assault. But what followed during the next couple of weeks helps us really see the insanity of the disease.

Two weeks after being raped at gunpoint, Catherine returned to the scene of the crime. Why would a woman willingly return to see a man who had raped her? Because she wanted cocaine. Her craving was so bad that she went back to the dealer who had raped her in order to buy the coke she craved.

I treated a mother who has an adult son in his thirties. Her son has a serious problem with alcohol and crack cocaine. One night he was purchasing crack from a drug dealer who was standing on a corner with several of his cronies. This young man must have said something to provoke an attack because soon he found himself on the ground, trying to protect himself, as he absorbed more than fifty kicks to his head and body.

Crack typically makes one highly paranoid, and because the son had used prior to this beating, he was extremely paranoid and refused to go to the emergency room, fearing that he would be arrested. Instead he went home. When he walked in the door, his mother almost fainted. His face and head were grotesquely swollen, almost beyond recognition. He was seeing double, possibly suffering from a concussion and brain damage. Still he refused to go to the hospital because he was afraid he would be locked up because of drug abuse.

His mother and her ex-husband nursed him back to health during the next couple of days. Eventually he was taken to the hospital because his jaw was broken in several places. The surgeons had to wait for the enormous swelling to subside before they could surgically repair his jaw. They also had to monitor his vision very closely because there was concern that the beating had detached the retina in his right eye.

Finally they were able to perform the surgery and wired his jaw shut for three weeks. Shortly after his surgery, his mother invited me to come to their home to conduct an intervention. I had worked with this young man about a year prior to this traumatic beating for a short period of time. He seemed moved by the intervention, as people usually are when they are in a major crisis. He went to a few AA meetings during the next couple of days, but eventually he started drinking again. Even having his jaw wired shut didn't stop him from drinking beer. He just drank through a straw, and yes, once the wires were removed from his jaw, he returned to that infamous corner. Only three weeks had passed and he was back in the same area buying crack again. This time he stayed in his car. But after he shorted the dealer for twenty dollars, a violent car chase occurred. Eventually he was cornered on a dead-end street. The scene must have looked like something from a demolition derby. The dealer was smashing the rear end of his car into the driver's side of this young man's vehicle as hard as he could, while shouting out how he was going to kill him. Finally, the man escaped. This was yet another near-fatal experience related to his use of drugs, but even this second close call didn't stop him or alter the course of his problem.

The latest news is that he was arrested after five squad cars chased him in his car for several blocks because he had fled from the scene of an auto accident. Needless to say, he was loaded and drunk, which is why he fled. He has been sentenced to six months in jail.

All of these examples make one thing very clear: once addiction takes hold, we are no longer capable of functioning rationally. Addiction overrides our best thinking and even our basic instinct for self-preservation. It's more powerful than maternal instinct, more powerful than the fear of losing a medical license, losing a spouse and family, harming our liver beyond repair, or losing a job. It is more powerful than the fear of mental illness, and even more powerful than the fear of being sent to prison. The outcome is devastating for addicts and their families. Untreated alcoholics and addicts typically end up in an institution or dead.

Why are we, who suffer from addiction, powerless over this insidious and destructive illness? Science is beginning to unravel this mystery. As I described earlier, recent studies have revealed that the addict's brain changes through the use of drugs. The part of the brain that changes is located near the reward center. At first, we decide to use, but then the brain takes over. This is why willpower is irrelevant.

The question of willpower often comes up in my sessions when a loved one or family member of an alcoholic or addict is trying to understand powerlessness. "I just don't understand why he can't just say no to drugs" is the concern often raised by a spouse or curious child. Powerlessness is hard to understand if you have not had personal experience with addiction. Our society does not acknowledge powerlessness. Our culture is based on a "can do" attitude. "You can do anything you set your mind to" is the promise our society holds up to those desiring a better life. But this thinking doesn't work when dealing with addiction.

My dear friend Father Martin, a Jesuit priest, used the following analogy to describe the process. He would say that if we have ever suffered from diarrhea, we have firsthand knowledge of being powerless. No matter what we say to ourselves, if we are not near a restroom when the urge comes over us, then we are likely to suffer an embarrassing moment. Nothing in the world we can do will stop our body from releasing its cargo. Anti-diarrhea medication may help, but our willpower—our desire to stop—is useless.

When it comes to addiction, we must discover and access a power greater than ourselves. We must be willing to do things 180 degrees different from what we have been doing. We need to have nothing short of a total commitment to recovery. If we are not 110 percent committed to our recovery, our efforts will most likely result in relapse.

A total commitment to recovery means that we are *willing to go to any lengths* to stay clean and sober. We need a commitment of this depth because the road that lies ahead of us isn't easy to travel. If we are less than totally committed, our attempt to stay clean and sober will falter. We will give up when things get tough, when they don't work out as planned, or when they don't work out as we hoped they would.

One of the deadliest expectations in early recovery is that others will applaud our efforts to stay clean and sober. Many of us hope that we will be immediately forgiven for past actions. This is a setup. More often than not, newly clean-and-sober alcoholics or addicts are met by their loved ones with skepticism, distrust, and suspiciousness. We want to forget that we have disappointed those close to us over and over again, but they remember.

If we are in recovery for the wrong reasons, we will be upset and disappointed by their reactions. If we feel this way and are considering giving up, then we have lost sight of the fact that we are getting well for our own benefit and not for the approval or recognition of others. Hopefully we are getting help because we are sick and tired of living the kind of life we have been living. Hopefully we will appreciate and value our recovery for everything it is to us, nothing more or less. Eventually we will have the opportunity to restore the trust we have betrayed in our relationships, but this takes time and a focused and consistent effort to work our program.

The bottom line is that our recovery is more important to us than it is to anyone else. If it's not, if we are expecting our wife or our husband or our children or our parents or our partner to appreciate what we are doing as much as or even more than we do, we are setting ourselves up for disappointment and trouble and possibly a relapse.

Going to any lengths to stay clean and sober is grounded in the idea that we are committed to taking total personal responsibility for our recovery. What do I mean by that? I mean that we are willing to take direction, get honest with ourselves, try new ways of functioning, and take whatever steps are necessary to stay clean and sober. This means that we are willing to call someone before we take the first drink, or use the first line of cocaine, or smoke the first joint, or take the first pill. This means that when we see ourselves building up to take a drink or use, we confront ourselves and "pull our own covers." When we take total responsibility for our recovery, we work the Twelve Steps and commit ourselves to discovering a spiritual solution to our problems.

This is at the heart of Step 3 of AA, "Made a decision to turn our will and our lives over to the care of God *as we understood Him.*" In this Step, we are making a conscious commitment to create a new way of life that is drug and alcohol free. We are making a commitment to find a spiritual solution to our personal problems, including our anxieties, depression, conflicts, relationships, and so on. We are making a commitment to get out of our way, give up our obsessions, and let go of our desire to control people, places, and things. The foundation of true recovery lies in humility.

Recovery is without doubt the road less traveled. It is a difficult road to follow—impossible if we are not 110 percent committed to the process. As if that isn't challenging enough, we are also faced with the reality that we need to make this commitment without a guarantee of the outcome. We need to trust the process, as we say in the program. And for us control freaks, this is not easy to do.

But there is something incredible that happens after we make this total commitment. The phenomenon is beautifully described by the famous author Johann Wolfgang von Goethe in his piece titled *On Commitment:*

> Until one is committed there is hesitancy, a chance to draw back, always ineffectiveness. Concerning all acts of initiative and creation there is one elementary truth, the ignorance of which kills countless ideas and splendid plans: that the moment one definitely commits oneself then Providence moves too. All sorts of things occur to help one that would never otherwise have occurred. A whole stream of events issues from the decision, raising in one's favor all manner of unforeseen incidents and meetings and material assistance which no man could have dreamed would come his way.

Stupid Thing 4

Being Selectively Honest

Recovery requires rigorous honesty. Nothing less will work.
We are as sick as we are secretive.

Honesty, open-mindedness, and willingness are essential for recovery. Previously, I discussed the importance of being open-minded and willing to go to any lengths for your recovery. In this chapter, I want to focus on self-honesty and why it is so necessary for recovery.

Alcoholism and other addictions feed on deceit, distrust, and dishonesty. We are driven to go to any lengths to drink or get high. We often violate personal values—no matter how strong or good they are—but not without consequence. For most of us, intense remorse, guilt, and shame are common underlying emotions. These feelings exacerbate the problem and make us drink or use more. At a deep level, most of us feel shame for who we are and what we have become. Author John Bradshaw refers to this as a *toxic shame.*

To develop a strong recovery, we need to be able to lance the boil and let all of the puss drain. We need to discuss all of the things that we don't want to talk about, especially our secrets—the things that we believe we would never share with anyone. This can be very difficult. We often cringe at this notion. It goes against everything we believed prior to recovery.

Our resistance is based on a misconception. What we thought was the appropriate way of being is not. What we believed to be in our best interest is not. Our experiences are like those of Alice in Wonderland, where everything that is, isn't and everything that isn't, is—where all the laws of logic and intuition are turned upside down. As addicts, our calibration is off. Something needs to change and that something is us. We are told on page 58 of the Big Book of AA that "Some of us have tried to hold on to our old ideas and the result was nil until we let go absolutely."

Most of us have been highly selective about what we are willing to share with others. False pride filters our self-disclosures. What typically happens before we disclose something personal, painful, or important is that it must pass through our censoring committee. The members of this group include self-hate, false pride, and the false self. The committee won't let anything be disclosed that could jeopardize this false image that must be maintained at all costs. We won't share much about our weaknesses when shame and self-doubt are telling us that we are less than other people because of these shortcomings. We are a prisoner of our false self, and most of the time, we don't even realize it.

At the heart of recovery lies the notion that we must challenge our old ideas, which are rooted in a faulty pride system. Neutralizing the power of false pride and loosening its control over our life is critical. These anachronisms need to be replaced by more effective principles of living.

There is a saying commonly heard in AA meetings: "You are as sick as you are secretive." The more open and honest we are, the more we heal. The more open we are, the more we are able to communicate. The more we share what we are ashamed of, the less power and control our false pride has in our life and the more serenity we experience. The more we "pull our own covers," the more humble we become.

We can think of the process of recovery as a salvage operation. We are recovering our lost self and sometimes discovering our true self. What we recover is our ability to be human. We have tried to be perfect and hold ourselves to an inhuman set of expectations. Recovery is about salvaging our humanity. We replace unreasonable expectations of perfection with an understanding of what it means to be human. We are not perfect; we are humans, being.

In order to begin this process, we need to undermine or neutralize the power of the addicted self and the tyranny of our false self. Self-honesty, born of necessity and pain, usually fuels this revolution. When we hit bottom and become sick and tired of being sick and tired, we are forced to see ourselves as we are instead of perpetuating the illusion that we hoped was true.

Once the crack in our false self has occurred, we automatically begin the process of searching for and developing our true, or real, self. Think of this as finding our spiritual self.

Understanding, respecting, and being responsive to this true, or spiritual, self is what integrity is all about. Another way of thinking about recovery is that it is establishing and maintaining integrity. I use the word *integrity* here to mean wholeness, a process in which we are committed to respecting our true, or spiritual, self. Maintaining integrity and wholeness is based on our ability to be honest with ourselves. We need to be honest about what is important to us and what we need. While this may seem simple, it is not an easy thing to accomplish. Many personal and social forces make it difficult for us to be aware of what we need and what we want.

Deception and self-deceit are rampant in our society. They are determined both biologically, psychologically, and socially. Tricking and manipulating others is evident in all species. It can manifest itself in a passive or active form. For example, the color and shape of the praying mantis looks like a part of a branch on a tree, which allows it to deceive its prey and be a more effective predator. Primates have been observed manipulating each other for mating purposes. Deceiving each other for personal ends is commonplace. The truth is that everyone in our society lies to one degree or another. In fact, lying is so pervasive that some human behavior scientists have developed categories for lies according to the underlying motivation.

Check out the following list: white lies (lies that lubricate social interaction), humorous lies (lies aimed at amusing the listener), altruistic lies (lies that are told to benefit someone else, reduce suffering, or increase self-esteem), defensive lies (lies that are told to protect oneself and others), aggressive lies (lies that are told in an effort to hurt someone else to gain an advantage for oneself), and pathological lies (lies that are told for no apparent reason—compulsive lying). Most of us are able to identify several situations in which we have behaved as described here.

While lies are rampant in our society, the lies that we tell to ourselves are the most self-destructive. Self-deception in all its various forms and manifestations is deadly because it undermines our ability to be honest with ourselves and attain humility. The capacity to be honest with ourselves is a necessary condition for recovery. We must get honest with ourselves if we are going to recover from our fatal disease.

Another problem with self-deceit is that it distorts our reality of what we need and want. I have seen some people try to present themselves to the world as devoid of any needs or personal desires. I have seen others present themselves as completely dependent on others, thinking that they must have someone's approval to survive. If life isn't working, then it may be that we are deceiving ourselves. Perhaps we are not facing who we really are and what we really want, and therefore, we develop an indirect way of trying to get the world to meet our needs. Let's look at why this happens.

We need to examine our level of awareness of our true needs. In order for me to tell you what I want, I need to have some idea of what is important to me. This is self-awareness, defined as the ability to know or have a sense of who we are and what we are experiencing. It means that we are present to our experience, our experience is personally accessible, and we are able to identify what we are experiencing. The "self" in this sense, and self-awareness, begin developing as a result of our childhood experiences.

If we were fortunate and had "good enough" parents who really empathized with us, we have a pretty good chance of starting out with a healthy core self. But rarely is this the case. We have all been subjected to injuries to our self-esteem from well-intentioned parents, teachers, relatives, and other caregivers. In fact, some behavioral scientists have argued that alcoholism and other addictions are "self disorders": drinking or using fills up the hole in our soul, covering up an emptiness caused by these wounds to our self-esteem, which gnaw at us.

Without an idea of who I am and what is important to me, I will be unable to be honest with you or myself. Let me give an example. I have been treating a woman who was neglected in her childhood. Her parents treated her as if she were invisible. Most of the things she asked for were ignored. The result of this kind of early childhood experience is that she learned to treat herself as invisible too. She has a difficult time identifying her feelings. If her husband, who comes to the sessions, is criticizing her or berating her, she is often speechless. It's not because she is afraid to speak up; she's not. She doesn't know what she is experiencing and therefore has nothing to say to her husband during these tense moments. But she is responding well to therapy, and her sense of what she is experiencing and her ability to put a label on her feelings has created a major breakthrough in her life and in her marriage. Now when he talks to her critically, she is able to speak up for herself and tell him what she wants and how she feels. She has recovered her own voice.

The next important issue to discuss is self-worth. Do I feel worthy of your time or interest? Do I feel worthy of recovery? Do I deserve to be loved or successful? Do I believe that you really care for me or that you are sincerely interested in what is important to me?

Here we see another result of an emotional injury to our self-esteem. If our parents didn't celebrate our existence, if they didn't authentically enjoy our spirit and energy, if they didn't see worth in us, then we suffered a self-worth injury. Our self-worth became fragile, unstable, and shaky. We have trouble telling others what we really think or how we really feel because we don't feel worthy. We erase our needs and place the needs of others far in front of our own.

Paradoxically, I believe it is this kind of injury that drives much of the self-centered and selfish behavior that I see in people who suffer from alcoholism and other addictions. Deep inside the person who has a self-worth wound is the belief that no one really cares and that he must manipulate others to get what he needs. I met Mike when he had completed thirty days of inpatient treatment. He was a very engaging young man who almost died from his addiction. All of Mike's needs were labeled as selfish when he was growing up. His parents weren't able to help him discriminate between selfish needs/wants and human needs/wants. So in recovery he was perplexed. He knew he had some human needs and wants—the desire to be of value to others, the need to be in a relationship, the need to make a difference, the need for growth and spirituality—but he didn't know how to separate these needs from more self-centered needs such as the need to be right or the need to be the center of attention. This problem was the direct result of a self-worth wound.

Later on in this book, I will discuss the difference between self-concern and selfishness, but for now, all I want to say is that what we think is selfish behavior may be falsely labeled.

The third issue of importance here is the ability to communicate with another person on an intimate and personal level. I refer to this as *personal language.* This relates to how well we can find words that truly reflect and help us express what we are experiencing or thinking. Our personal language is determined by our level of self-awareness (our ability to identify what we want), whether we feel worthy enough to express our personal desire, and whether we can support ourselves in the process. Personal language is rarely taught or encouraged. In fact, much of our childhood discourages it. During my own childhood, I was often *told* how I was feeling, what should be important, how much I should eat. This was a far cry from being encouraged to *talk* about what was important to me or to find the words that might have helped heal the painful loss of my father when I was eleven years old.

So these three things—undeveloped self-awareness, a sense of unworthiness, and poorly developed personal language—make it hard for us to share what we need and what is important to us.

In order for us to develop integrity, we have to identify the ways that we deceive, which will help us become rigorously honest. This is quite a challenge because we don't have a very good sense of who we really are and what is truly important to us. We feel unworthy of success—let alone another person's true interest and concern—and we don't have the ability to find the words that will help us talk about our pain or other important and personal topics. Sounds pretty hopeless, doesn't it? Well it isn't. We are in need of a personal overhaul. There is no denying it. But we are not hopeless. We can heal these wounds and learn how to support ourselves, soothe our anxiety, and lick our own wounds. We can grow up.

Recovery is an initiation into life. If we stay the course, we will grow up and learn how to take care of ourselves. No one is perfect, and if we try to have the perfect program, we will end up miserable in recovery. Our humility, open-mindedness, and willingness are the keys to our spiritual growth.

Stupid Thing 5
Feeling Special and Unique

Humility is the spiritual foundation of recovery. In order to feel worthy, we do not need to be unique. People who do best in recovery are those who surrender and follow suggestions.

A common first response to the requirements of recovery is to negotiate, to pick and choose what we think will be helpful. One person might say, "I don't need to go to a meeting every day for the first ninety days of recovery. Two meetings a week are plenty enough for me." Another newcomer might exclaim, "I don't need a sponsor. I can do this by myself." And yet another might say, "I don't have to work all the Steps. One and Twelve are enough for me." This kind of thinking is based on the mistaken belief that we are special and unique and that we don't have to do what everyone else has done to develop a solid, robust recovery. This dangerous attitude has led many newcomers, and even some old-timers, back into the depths of despair and relapse. We are special and unique, but not in this sense.

To begin recovery, we need to surrender. Surrender can be best defined as the total and complete acceptance of the reality of our situation. We suffer from an illness that we are powerless to defeat on our own. Surrender also means that we accept that our illness has impaired the way we manage our life.

This is a lot to accept if we are governed by false pride and have a tendency to minimize the severity of problems. The motivation behind this self-defeating strategy is "If I don't have to do everything that everyone else has to do, then I am not as sick or as bad as all of those who need to work the whole program." Here is where the danger begins. If we do not surrender to the reality of our condition, then we will not be moved or motivated to go to any lengths to stay clean and sober. We will not have the necessary foundation to tackle the upcoming tasks that are necessary to establish a solid recovery.

If we truly accept that we suffer from a fatal illness over which we are powerless, we will experience what is called an *existential crisis*. An existential crisis occurs when we let go of an unhealthy behavior, but we don't yet have a better and healthier alternative available. We are betwixt and between. We are in limbo. We'll want to avoid the feelings that surface from being in such a difficult position, but it is important to feel the desperation and anxiety that come from surrender. An existential crisis places us at a crossroads between complete despair and hope. Allowing ourselves to surrender to this crisis shifts something inside of us. We become open to new possibilities; our reliance on our false self is shattered. This prepares us for the next step in recovery: *hope.*

Hope is a therapeutic force present in all forms of healing. Hope springs from faith at this stage of recovery: a faith that there is a better and healthier alternative. We find our hope in the Twelve Steps. On page 58 of the Big Book, the newcomer is told that "Rarely have we seen a person fail who has thoroughly followed our path." If we believe ourselves to be special, then we won't adhere to these crucial words of advice.

How do we develop faith? For those of us in recovery, faith comes from witnessing the transformation in others who suffer from a similar problem. Through attendance at Twelve Step meetings, we witness firsthand the miracle called recovery. We see other people who are suffering from this terrible illness successfully trudging the road of recovery. It is by witnessing recovery firsthand that the seed of hope is planted.

So give up this nonsense that you need to be special. My clinical supervisor William C. Rader, M.D., a truly gifted psychiatrist, provided me with the following analogy. He used to say that when we undergo a surgical procedure, we don't want to be special; we want to be average. Average patients do well in most surgical procedures; the special cases run into trouble. Special cases typically do not survive. In recovery, it's okay to be average. We want to be in the middle of the pack. The average person in AA gets well. The special person doesn't because he or she doesn't do what the average AA member does to stay sober. This sabotages recovery and usually ends up causing chronic relapses.

Feeling that we are special also prevents us from attaining humility. Humility is the spiritual foundation of our recovery, and the only solution to the medical problem of addiction is a spiritual cure.

Stupid Thing 6

Not Making Amends

To develop a strong spiritual foundation for recovery,
it is essential that we accept full responsibility for
our harmful and hurtful behavior and that we attempt
to repair the damage that we have caused
in our relationships with family, friends, and loved ones.

We will face many difficult tasks in the process of recovery. Life is difficult. This is the baseline from which all else follows. When we accept life for what it is, we give up fighting. We surrender and accept the extent and severity of our dilemma: we are powerless over alcohol and other drugs and our life has become unmanageable. When we surrender, we develop a belief that we can find a better way of life, accept the reality that we are unable to get well on our own, and make a commitment to finding new solutions to our problems. If we have done this, then we have many of the attitudes and perspectives necessary to tackle the difficult challenges that lie ahead in recovery.

One of the greatest challenges in recovery is taking responsibility for our harmful and hurtful behavior and making amends to those whom we love and whom we have hurt. This action is essential if we are going to enjoy all of the benefits and promises of recovery. Amends are also necessary if we wish to reestablish trust.

In order to propel us and our families toward healing, our amends have to come from a deep empathy for how our illness has affected those we love. Our amends need to emerge from a deep understanding of the *spiritual wound* that we have inflicted on those we love and care about. Unfortunately, many balk at this difficult task. Why is it so difficult to take responsibility for our harmful and hurtful behaviors?

The answer lies in understanding the ruthless control that false pride has in our life. If we continue to allow false pride to determine what we do and don't do, then it will interfere and impede making amends and stop us from accepting total responsibility for our hurtful and insensitive behavior. Let's explore the psychology underlying the difficulty of personal responsibility for alcoholics and addicts.

Most alcoholics and addicts have developed extensive psychological mechanisms to avoid and deflect taking personal responsibility. One tried-and-true approach is the *tit-for-tat mentality.* The tit-for-tat mentality is typical with couples in the early stages of recovery. The addict's role in this destructive pattern of communication is to justify all of his or her behavior, blaming the rotten behavior on the spouse. "I wouldn't act this way if you hadn't provoked me!" becomes the battle cry for the addict in all kinds of situations, regardless of his or her culpability.

The tit-for-tat mentality is designed to rationalize and justify our behavior so we can falsely conclude that we don't have any personal responsibility in the present situation. Here are some of the more common tit-for-tat maneuvers:

- "If you wouldn't criticize me, I wouldn't drink."
- "Nothing I do for you is ever enough! That's why I get so angry."

- "You keep this home such a mess. I can't stand being around anymore. That's why I stay out late at night."
- "If you would show more interest in what I do, I would want to be around you more."
- "If you wanted to have sex more frequently, I would be much happier."
- "If you appreciated what I do for you, our relationship would be much better."
- "If you would only cherish me, then I wouldn't feel so jealous around other women."

The list can go on and on, and it usually does. Unfortunately, couples who are trapped in this loop have a difficult time breaking free because there is usually a kernel of truth in the other person's complaint. We are influenced and affected by our partner's behavior. This doesn't mean, however, that we can justify our behavior because of our partner's behavior, especially if we want a better relationship.

The tit-for-tat mentality indicates that we are suffering from emotional dependency—this is the kernel of truth. We end up being highly reactive to our partner because he or she is too important to us. We depend on our partner's approval, validation, and behavior for our security, prestige, self-esteem, and happiness. The degree to which we are caught in this deadly game reflects our level of emotional maturity. So when we find ourselves justifying our behavior because of what our partner is or isn't doing, then we are playing tit-for-tat. This mentality won't lead to a solution, no matter how hard we try to convince our partner that he or she is the problem.

Another powerful way addicts avoid taking responsibility for unhealthy behavior is what I call the *Houdini maneuver.* While the tit-for-tat mentality justifies hurtful behavior because "You made me treat you this way because of how you behaved," the Houdini approach is more sophisticated. This technique is designed to create an illusion by instilling confusion and doubt in the person with whom we are interacting. Doubt and confusion are created by challenging the other person's reality at every turn of the page. The essence of this powerful interpersonal tactic is simple: "What seems to be true is only an illusion." Alcoholics and addicts go to great lengths to turn things around or invert the truth. Just ask one of their partners. The co-alcoholic or co-addict enters recovery uncertain of reality because of the years that he or she has listened to and been influenced by the Houdini approach. The effect of this maneuver is that alcoholics and addicts never take responsibility for their behavior because they believe their partner is always wrong. Addicts don't hesitate to turn things around to unequivocally demonstrate their point. So the addict is off the hook, and a flailing, confused co-addict remains dangling on the hook expertly placed in his or her mouth.

Addicts employ many other maneuvers in weaving this web of deceit to deflect personal responsibility, but they are not the only ones playing this deadly game. Spouses and partners are usually as adroit at these ploys. The point is that we all have difficulty taking total, and I mean *total*, responsibility for our life. So here is the bottom line: *We do what we do because of who we are, not because of someone else's behavior. We are responsible for our life, for our feelings, for our actions, for our self-esteem, for our beliefs, and for our response to those things that are out of our control. If we are overly influenced by our partner's behavior, then we need to take responsibility for that too, which means learning how to stand on our own two feet, grow up emotionally, and learn how to support ourselves to become the person we want to be.*

Now that we are aware of some of the ways we avoid personal responsibility, I want to spend the remainder of this chapter discussing what it means to truly make amends to our partner or our family.

When we finally face the reality of how we have behaved, we see that we have spiritually wounded those people we love the most. This is not easy because it means facing a part of ourselves that we are ashamed of: the *despised self*. But if we do not face this part of ourselves, it will continue to control us from behind the scenes.

We need to take this difficult step very seriously. There is a reason that people used to drop to their knees when apologizing. It symbolized their humility and deep recognition of their transgression. When we can face how we have spiritually wounded those we care about, we are ready to make amends. We need to consider getting on our knees when we make our amends. From our knees, we can discuss the nature of our wrongs, our remorse and sorrow, our recognition of how we have spiritually wounded someone, and how we propose to be accountable for our actions. We ask the person whether anything has been overlooked. We encourage the person to be forthcoming. And finally, we ask whether the person believes the apology, whether he or she believes our sincerity. If we are found to be insincere, we ask what it was about the apology that gave that impression. Be open to the response. If there is validity to what the person says, we apologize for that too and make a commitment to return at some future date to restate the amends. Then we need to get to work on what blocked us from being sincere.

Many of us might say, "That is quite an order. How can anyone go through with that?" The truth is there are countless men and women who have made their amends and who have discovered the emotional freedom in their lives and the increase in their self-esteem that come from taking responsibility and being accountable for their actions. This is a real possibility. But we will have to face our demons and dethrone our false pride to realize it. I hope that most of us will choose to walk this road less traveled.

Stupid Thing 7
Using the Program to Try to Become Perfect

Most of our life has been spent trying to be perfect.
This has been a spurious goal. Instead we need to learn
how to become more human.

Believe it or not, perfectionism underlies most of our problems. When confronted with this, many of my patients say, "Doc, you're nuts. I am not a perfectionist. I rarely do anything perfectly." The problem for perfectionists is not that they do everything perfectly, but that they feel that things should be done perfectly. The problem is related to the standards we impose on our behavior, thoughts, feelings, values, and actions. This doesn't mean that we are able to live up to these standards. Oftentimes we *can't* live up to these impossible demands, and that is where our problems begin. Let me clarify how perfectionism develops and how it plays itself out in our life.

Karen Horney, M.D., a brilliant psychiatrist, posited that at a very early age we make a decision that we should be perfect. This decision is driven by a basic anxiety that we won't be loved. Given the fact that we have the longest period of infant dependency of any species on the planet, the anxiety engendered by the belief that we won't be loved is quite compelling. We erroneously conclude that if we are perfect, which each of us uniquely defines, we will always be loved and therefore always feel secure.

So we create an idealized self, a self-concept that is constructed on the fragile skeleton of perfectionism. To ensure that we act according to its specifications, we develop a pride system that imposes the necessary values and punishments.

Our pride system imposes a set of *shoulds* on our behavior to support the realization of the idealized self. We should do, feel, and think this way or that way, and when we don't, there's quite a price to pay. Our pride system unleashes guilt, shame, and self-hate to ensure our compliance with the rules it was made to uphold. The problem lies in the goal of perfectionism. We pressure ourselves to be perfect at any price, and we demand nothing less. Each of us reacts to this self-imposed pressure in different ways. Some of us believe that we can pull it off, and we impart on a crusade to become perfect. Or we become self-effacing and spend our entire life putting ourselves down in the spirit of perfection. Sometimes we resign and give up on life altogether. While some of these adaptations are more socially acceptable than others, like the aggressive businessman or the self-effacing wife, they are all maladaptive because they are based on the myth of perfection.

Can you see the role this pressure plays when a person has a problem with alcohol and other drugs? I can see it clearly in my life. I turned to alcohol and other drugs to bolster my ability to live up to the unrealistic standards I set for myself: impossible standards that left me feeling inadequate, defective, ashamed, and yet entitled. Drugs removed these feelings of inadequacy, and drugs kept the incongruity between who I thought I should be and who I am to a dull, throbbing pain. Once I stopped using drugs one day at a time, I had an opportunity to face these demons. But they are persistent little devils, which followed me right into recovery.

In retrospect, I can see that I started to use the Twelve Steps of AA to accomplish what I failed at before. Armed with all of recovery's new and powerful information, I erroneously believed I could finally pull off this perfect thing. Yes, I was one of those people at the AA meetings that you hate. I worked the "perfect AA program," and I was all too willing to let you know how you, too, could have "perfect sobriety" if you followed my advice. I was the egomaniac with an insecurity complex. Life was black and white, as it always is when this process in involved. There was no gray at all, except when a gray cloud surrounded me after I did something less than perfect.

I was deluded with my self-importance. But the truth was that no one expected me to work a perfect program. My sponsor didn't demand it from me; it was my trip. It's amazing how grandiosity seems to live side by side so comfortably with feelings of inadequacy and shame. I've come to realize that these two states are often strange but common roommates. I don't remember exactly how it happened, but one day I had an "aha" experience when I realized that I was doing the same thing in recovery that I did before recovery: trying to be perfect.

It was then that I realized what the problem had been all along. I wanted to be perfect because, in some distorted way, I truly believed that being human wasn't good enough. What a corner I had painted myself into! I was human, which wasn't good enough; I wasn't perfect, which was also unacceptable. This was the ultimate in self-alienation. It's no wonder that life sucked and I needed to get high.

It was then I started to dig deep down into my self-rejection. This journey has taken me in many different directions that are beyond the scope of this chapter. Let me just say that I realized I was dealing with a multilayered problem. I had to face not only the dysfunction in my family of origin but also the absurd ideas our culture has of what it means to be a man. As I trudged this therapeutic trail, I started to really make some significant strides in emotional sobriety. I began to uncover and confront why I had rejected myself, and after several years of going to therapy and reworking the Twelve Steps, I began to embrace and honor my humanity. Today I strive to be what I am: a human being, perfectly imperfect.

I hope I will always remember what my mentor, Walter Kempler, M.D., a pioneer in family therapy, used to say: "There is nothing wrong with striving for perfection, as long as we realize that we will never attain it." This and other realizations, along with a healthy dose of personal acceptance, have created a level of peace and serenity I had only dreamed of. There is much work that still lies ahead for me in terms of dealing with my emotional immaturity, but I have taken several important steps on this journey. I hope you will choose to do the same.

Stupid Thing 8
Confusing Self-Concern with Selfishness

Self-concern is different from selfishness. It does not exclude others; it is inclusive. Part of our self is concerned with cooperating with and pleasing others. These desires are natural and healthy, when they are balanced with our personal integrity.

Anyone who has spent time in AA or other Twelve Step–based recovery programs realizes that self-centeredness and self-will run riot are viewed as the root cause of addiction. Many Twelve Steppers interpret this as meaning concern with personal needs is "bad." There seems to be no room for self with the capital *S* or lowercase *s* in recovery. They think self in any shape or form is a demon that needs to be exorcised. The myth perpetuated by this notion is that becoming "selfless" is the primary goal in recovery.

While it's important for us to put "self" into a healthier perspective, we also need to learn how to take better care of ourselves. Many of us become self-centered because we don't know how to take care of ourselves emotionally, spiritually, or interpersonally. We are ignorant of how to stay centered in relationships and soothe ourselves when anxious, disappointed, or concerned. The concept about self that is bantered around in many AA circles perpetuates this myth and can be problematic for several reasons, which I hope will become clear in this chapter.

If you look at how our society and culture shape personal development, I believe you will agree with the following conclusion: there is a conspiracy at work in our society aimed at alienating you from your true self. The alienation from your true self begins at birth. Following are several examples.

Many well-intentioned parents are encouraged to place their infant on a feeding schedule. The child is fed when the plan dictates, not when the child's biology requires. If a child needs to cry or rage, he or she is often discouraged from such displays because of the parent's social or personal discomfort. At school, the active child must learn to suppress his or her excitement and assimilate into the passive learning environment that characterizes most educational approaches today. We are cajoled, manipulated, and sometimes coddled away from our core self in order to fit some idea of what society says we should be. We are conditioned to fit into the social norm, which too often means fragmenting and splitting ourselves into pieces so we can gain social approval. Some social critics have referred to this conditioning as creating a hypnotic trance. We are asleep, dreaming we are awake.

We have contributed to our problem by buying into these myths. We are simultaneously victims and perpetrators of this psychological crime. We disown many important and vital parts of ourselves to fit in and be what we think we should be. We collude with society and our parents and join the fatal conspiracy. We become as much to blame as our parents, well-intentioned caregivers, grandparents, teachers, mentors, lovers, spouses, colleagues, and bosses. We alienate our true self over and over again, often to the point where our true self is unrecognizable. We don't know our self except through the roles that we play.

This perspective offers an intriguing way of understanding mental illness and personal distress. Our personal level of suffering is related to the degree of alienation from our true self. Another way of saying the same thing is that our level of "dis-ease" is related to how fragmented or disconnected we are—how cut off we are—from our true self.

Recovery is a salvage operation. We are actually recovering our lost self: disowned and fragmented parts of our being. In order to become whole, we need to integrate all aspects of our self.

Another way to describe the process of recovery is to think about it as recovering our emotional and spiritual development. Most of us were developmentally arrested at a pretty early age because of our addiction. Recovery helps us reclaim and integrate the lessons we never completed.

Let's discuss a specific issue that we all have to face. There are two powerful forces within us that are usually in conflict: our desire to please and our individuality. We become selfish or we become people-pleasers. Often, we don't know how to honor both of these desires simultaneously.

Let's discuss the nature of these two forces. First is our desire to please and cooperate. We all have a desire to please those who are important to us, to cooperate with them, and to join or unite with them. We are social animals and we thrive in union. Recent surveys of the medical and sociological literature have demonstrated the importance of love for survival. If we are in a loving relationship, we live longer, recover faster and better from physical illnesses, commit fewer crimes, and make a better living.

I believe this desire to please and cooperate is hardwired in our DNA. In our infancy, we need our attachment to our parents to survive. This desire to please and cooperate reinforces this bonding, which in turn increases our chance for survival. When the parent-child bond is tenuous or unstable, there are grave consequences for development. For instance, there is a much greater chance for parents to abuse their child if they didn't bond with their child or if the bonding was interrupted at childbirth.

The second force in our life is our desire to follow our own song, to pursue our individuality, and to seek personal mastery. This force is also necessary for our survival, as it moves us to become the best person we can be. This is a growth force that moves us forward in our development and maturity.

For most of us, the desire to please and individuality are forces in conflict throughout our life and throughout our intimate relationships. We do not know how to please without losing ourselves; we do not know how to stay connected to our parents or a partner without losing our individuality; or we do not know how to cooperate with our parents or a partner while staying centered. What we do is fall out of one side of the bed or the other. We try to please and cooperate by submitting to our parents' or our partner's will, or we try to control them and get them to submit to our demands. We may distance ourselves, run away, detach, split, disconnect, and/or become emotionally withdrawn, building a stone wall. When we fail to integrate our desire to please and our individuality, we are not acting out of integrity. When we are not centered, we react and let the pull of our emotional fusion to our parents or our partner control our response, regardless of whether we are trying to please or detach.

When we emotionally withdraw, it is hard for us to recognize that we are being controlled by an emotional connection. We think we are acting independently. Independence is not individuality. When we pull away because of our emotional dependency, we are in fact being controlled by these feelings. The emotional dependency is forcing us to withdraw.

This is what I believe happens when a person is being selfish.

When we use independence to deal with emotional dependency, we are being selfish. We think we are honoring our individuality, but we are not. This is pseudo-independence. It is not an independence grounded in individuality. It is a reaction to the pull of our emotional dependency. Few of us want to be controlled, and we go to any lengths to avoid it. We just don't realize that what is happening within us makes us feel controlled. Instead we externalize the blame, which keeps us ignorant of the real problem. The real problem is our emotional dependency on others and how we are controlled by this dependency, by this self-imposed pressure. Selfishness is pseudo-independence intended to neutralize emotional dependency. The drive toward self-realization—integrating apparently conflicting aspects of ourselves—is so deep and powerful that when ignored, it lets us know by causing us serious emotional, physical, or spiritual problems.

To achieve real emotional maturity, we need to honor everything that is important to us, and this includes our desire to cooperate and our need to be ourselves. When we consciously balance these two forces, we are functioning with integrity and wholeness. We self-actualize. We strive for balance and we strive to stay centered when facing conflicts. We strive to honor our own personal desires and the personal desires of our partner. When conflict occurs, as it inevitably will, we maintain our connection. We don't submit to them, try to control them, or run away emotionally or physically. This healthy tension creates real maturity and is one of the life lessons we missed. My mentor Dr. Walter Kempler used to refer to this process as "all hands on deck."

Confusing selfishness with self-concern cuts the legs out from under us. The confusion becomes self-defeating and self-destructive. It prevents us from acting on our own behalf, lest we be selfish. Self-concern is not selfishness! When we honor ourselves, our existence, our life, we are not being selfish. Learning to honor and care for ourselves is a hallmark of recovery.

When we honor ourselves, we strive to function with integrity and honor all of our personal desires. We strive to please others and honor our feelings simultaneously. We strive to assert ourselves appropriately, but not at anyone's expense. We strive to stay balanced and take responsibility for our feelings and personal desires rather than manipulate and maneuver others to take care of us and make us feel all right. We seek to be of value without losing ourselves in the process. When we take care of ourselves, we learn to stand on our own two feet. The result of these efforts is peace of mind and serenity, what Bill Wilson referred to as "emotional sobriety." This, too, is possible in our life if we strive to remain conscious and work our program. There are many long-timers who have trudged this road and are more than honored to help us along the way.

Stupid Thing 9
Playing Futile Self-Improvement Games

Recovery requires honesty. Playing games with ourselves is dishonest and doesn't address our problems. It is instead a sophisticated strategy to avoid dealing with our problems. Avoidance is ultimately destructive to the process of recovery.

One of the most important skills in recovery is self-honesty. It is stated on page 58 of the Big Book that even those "who suffer from grave emotional and mental disorders . . . recover if they have the capacity to be honest." It is common knowledge that if we have the capacity to be introspective, without avoiding those things about ourselves that we do not like and that we do not want to see, then we have a good chance of developing a solid program of recovery. Most of us who are now trudging the road of recovery have made a career out of self-deception. We have not been honest with ourselves and others because it has been too painful. We have run from the truth, distorted the truth, and twisted reality over and over again. We have mastered the art of self-deception.

Recovery is the antithesis of addiction. If addiction is characterized by deceit and self-deception, then recovery is characterized by openness and honesty. In recovery, we shift our behavior 180 degrees. We do the opposite of what we used to do. Keep this in mind for the remainder of this chapter. Be open-minded and keep an open heart. Fight the temptation to run away. There may be some things I discuss that may be difficult to face. Remember, in honesty there is freedom. So here we go!

I am convinced if we are honest with ourselves—really honest with ourselves—we will see that we play games. I do, and you do too. We all have a racket. We play games with ourselves and with others. We may not realize it, but these games keep us stuck. They keep us emotionally immature and emotionally dependent on others. Typically the games we play are designed to manipulate others for emotional support, indirectly extract approval from others, or inflate our self-esteem at their expense. Here are a few of the more common games that people play:

- *Helpless Harry.* Helpless Harry comes across as incapable of thinking for himself. He is a follower and doesn't know what to do without getting advice or approval for his decisions. Harry doubts everything he does. He fools himself and others into thinking he is incompetent and incapable of coping with life. His pseudo-helplessness is a ruse designed to get other people to think for him and tell him what to do. Harry doesn't want to make his own decisions because he might be wrong. Harry doesn't want to take a risk, so he plays it safe and gets other people to think for him. Because Harry is a master at this game, he successfully gets well-intentioned therapists and friends to take responsibility for his decisions. Unfortunately, Harry never grows up. He sabotages his emotional and spiritual development through manipulating others to make his decisions and provide him with emotional support for his actions.

- ***Bertha the Bear Trapper.*** Bertha's entire goal in life is to be able to say, "Gotcha!" It's all about being one up in her relationships. Bertha's approach is quite clever: she pretends that she needs help or advice, but as soon as you advise her, she rejects it and argues with you. Bertha really doesn't want advice; Bertha wants you to feel impotent. Her goal is to make others feel powerless because that is what she really feels deep down within. So she sets up her traps and catches well-intentioned do-gooders all day long by playing her game of rejecting their help.

- ***Self-Effacing Sam.*** Sam's game is always to be wrong. Sam lives his life constantly apologizing for his existence, regardless of whether he has done something wrong or not. No matter the discussion, Sam is always finding fault with himself. He is always wrong, inadequate, or incapable. Sam's ploy is to manipulate others into telling him what a wonderful person he truly is by telling everyone what a loser or incompetent person he thinks he is. This kind of game makes it difficult for anyone to be truly angry with Sam. How can you be upset with someone who is constantly putting himself down? This is one of the benefits of the game that Sam is playing. It keeps people from being upset with him, because after all, who can kick a good man while he is down?

In addition to these types of games, many people in recovery play what I call *recovery games.* These games have the same goals as those described above. The difference is that the person who plays recovery games uses therapy or a Twelve Step program to camouflage the true purpose of the game. Here are a few common recovery games:

- ***Spiritual Sally.*** Spiritual Sally avoids life by hiding behind her commitment to living a spiritual life. Whenever Sally runs into difficulty in a relationship, she hides behind her spirituality by becoming ultra-righteous. She takes the position that if her partner worked a better spiritual program, there would be no problem in the relationship. It's everyone's fault but Sally's. If only the world were as spiritual as she is, there would be no conflict. Here's an example: Jane is twelve years sober and works very hard in her recovery. She has a very personal relationship with God as she understands him and readily shares at meetings about the value of her conscious contact with her Higher Power. Jane came to therapy with her boyfriend, Terry, who was then sober for five years. Terry and Jane were becoming more serious about their relationship and problems started surfacing, as they often do. As a person becomes more important to us, the relationship becomes more difficult. Jane and Terry's problems were related to how they were dealing with conflict. Here's what typically happened. Whenever Terry confronted Jane about something he didn't like, she withdrew. Terry confronted Jane about her insistence that they should always go to separate AA meetings. Terry believed that this was a good idea the majority of the time, but he wanted to attend some meetings with her. Jane would tell Terry that this wasn't a good idea. She stated with authority that it wouldn't be good for their programs. When Jane was confronted by Terry for dismissing his idea and not considering his position, she withdrew and refused to talk further. What she did next is at the core of this game: *she told him that once he had more recovery, he would understand.* Instead of looking at how she was withdrawing and one-upping Terry, she disguised her behavior as healthier than his, which justified her stonewalling. This put her partner in a very difficult spot. He had trouble challenging what she was doing to him because he respected her recovery. I am not saying that we should never detach or separate during the heat of battle in a relationship. There are times when this is healthy, but only if we stay connected during the process. If we take a time-out because we need it, that's fine, but if we try to convince our partner that we're taking a time-out because they need it, it is unhealthy. In a healthy relationship, we take care of ourselves and encourage our partner to do the same. Those weren't the rules that Jane was playing by. Simply stated, she was letting Terry know that he was wrong and she was right. She was self-righteous and trying to convince Terry to do what she wanted. When we play this game, we camouflage our true intentions behind a cloak of spirituality. I am not suggesting that Jane should go to meetings with Terry. She has every right to tell Terry how she feels, as long as she does so without trying to convince Terry that she is right. She has every right to say she doesn't want to go to meetings with him. But I'm criticizing the way she communicated her position. She dismissed Terry's feelings by implying that he wasn't sober long enough. This is nonsense. She would be on healthier ground if she just stated her position and recognized his disappointment and his desire to share their experience in recovery together. This is very different from manipulating Terry. So if we are in a situation like this, be straight. Even if we think our position is unreasonable, it is important to stand for it rather than hide it. At least we are being authentic.

- *Next Time Ian.* Ian's game is to do better next time. He lives in the future. Ian can justify any rotten behavior because he "will do better next time." Ian lives his life by making promises about the future. He doesn't really change his behavior because he is never honest with himself or truly accountable for his actions. He avoids taking responsibility for what he is doing right now by making promises about the future. He is always leaving the moment and living in the future. Ian tries to get you to buy into his promises and let him off the hook for his current transgressions without ever changing a single thing. The bottom line for Ian is that if he says, "I'll do better next time," then others can't be upset with him and hold him accountable for his actions. Doing better next time is like the get-out-of-jail-free card in Monopoly. Ian uses it whenever he is in a jam. The problem here is that he is never making proper amends; he is only saying he is sorry, so appropriate action never follows. He is all talk and no action. I often tell my patients who are struggling in a relationship with someone like Ian to watch the person's feet rather than listen to his or her mouth. Action speaks louder than words. This is the criteria we need to use to judge Ian's sincerity. We can't talk ourselves out of the trouble that our behavior creates. We can only make amends.

- *AA Bob.* AA Bob's game is to have the best AA program in the community. Bob talks program all day and all night. He is a serious student of recovery and works hard at understanding it, but unfortunately Bob does not apply what he knows. His knowledge is not integrated into his behavior. He does not walk like he talks, but this is hard to see because Bob lives his life in AA meetings. In meetings, he is at the top of his game. He intellectually understands the principles of recovery and readily shares this knowledge with newcomers and long-timers alike. Bob is comfortable in meetings because he is the AA master, the all-knowing keeper of the secrets of recovery. Bob is proud of the fact that he usually attends more AA meetings than anyone else in recovery. However, if you take Bob out of an AA meeting and have him deal with the challenges and issues of an intimate relationship, he is lost. If he can't use an AA slogan or platitude to address the situation at hand, he becomes confused and uncertain. Bob's game is to use recovery to hide the fact that he is still feeling painfully inadequate. He looks great on the outside, but inside is another story. He is like the Wizard of Oz. He is omnipotent and omniscient, but behind the curtain, he is a man, no more and no less. Bob is hiding in AA. AA is his curtain and the meetings are his land of Oz. He doesn't really know how to apply the principles in all his affairs, and he is too ashamed to admit it. His false pride keeps him from stepping out from behind the curtain and facing the fact that he hasn't integrated the principles of the program into his life. He fools himself into thinking that he's "got it" when in fact he doesn't. This is not to say that Bob hasn't made substantial progress from where he was when he entered recovery, but he has further to go. His next step is to take the ideas he has about recovery and weave them into the fabric of his life.

- *Do It My Way Jeff.* Jeff is a bully in sheep's clothing. He bullies his friends and sponsees into doing things his way because he has more sobriety or recovery. Jeff acts like he knows what's best for everyone. He readily tells others what to do, how to behave, and what principles should govern their behavior, but he is unaware of the incongruities in his own behavior. He doesn't realize that he himself doesn't live up to the standards he sets for everyone else. Here's an example. I treated a man named Bill, who had a Jeff for a sponsor. Bill loved Jeff and found him helpful in many ways. However, when it came to helping Bill with the troubles he was having with his daughter and wife, Jeff became a bully. He would not listen to the terrible struggle that Bill was experiencing. His advice to Bill was black and white—do this or else you are not a good father. Jeff urged Bill to be responsive to his daughter's need at his wife's expense. Given the fact that she was a stepparent, this was the kiss of death. Misplaced loyalties in a blended family can cause serious problems, and Bill was definitely proving this to be true. His sponsor, Jeff, was exacerbating this couple's problems because of the type of advice he was giving. Jeff was unable to empathize with Bill's wife and therefore rarely considered her feelings when discussing her with Bill. When Bill questioned Jeff about the lopsided nature of his advice, Jeff became indignant and frustrated: "You obviously don't want to be a man." This shut Bill down and humiliated him. Jeff's words were sacred and therefore should not be challenged. Jeff didn't hesitate to let his newly sober charge know that he crossed the line when he challenged him. The Jeffs of this world are usually highly intellectual and skilled at using their intellect to manipulate and beat others into submission. If this doesn't work, they use their size or bravado to intimidate others to make them submit to their ideas. I don't want to convey the idea that the Jeffs in this world are unhelpful, because it's not true. They are quite helpful and insightful until you hit one of their blind spots. Then you realize that they aren't all-knowing. This is when sponsors can become dangerous. When a sponsor becomes a marriage counselor or therapist without credentials and proper training, the results can be tragic. So beware and understand that sponsors have blind spots and limitations too.

- *Let's Just Get Along Louise.* Louise wants everyone to be happy. Happy, happy, happy is what Louise tries to endorse, no matter the occasion. Louise is the recovery variation of Pollyanna. A Pollyanna can turn lead into gold by just looking at it. Louise is incredible at minimizing and understating problems. The truth is that Louise doesn't want to see things as they are because it means that she won't have any control and conflict may follow. Louise's game is to avoid conflict through niceties and by telling everyone that if they worked a better program, they wouldn't be angry, resentful, or argumentative. What Louise doesn't realize is that people can resolve feelings of anger and resentment. Louise is frightened by these emotions, so she attempts to avoid them by manipulating others to avoid conflict too. What a terrible curse this person suffers. She has been walking on eggshells her entire life.

- *Nothing Will Work Norman.* Norman is the ultimate pessimist. He doesn't want to believe that things in his life can be different because he protects himself from disappointment. He lowers his expectations for life in order to avoid disappointment and self-hate. He sees the glass as half empty rather than half full. He believes that optimistic people are unreasonable and labels them as unrealistic. He's depressed and difficult to hang out with because he is so negative. Norman has resigned. He has given up because he doesn't believe he can make life work, so he doesn't try. Norman is one of those people who are underachievers. Others see potential in him, but he doesn't acknowledge it himself. Norman has abandoned himself. He will never enjoy the promises of recovery.

These are just a few of the games that people play in recovery. Diagnose yourself. We know we are playing a futile self-improvement game if it results in a decrease of our personal freedom. Our game playing is based on a lack of faith in ourselves to be able to deal with life authentically, on life's terms. These games are self-defeating and self-limiting because they are designed to manipulate others for support or validation. When we manipulate others to do for us what we aren't doing for ourselves (even if we think we are involved in self-improvement), it will end up a disaster.

Games do not help us grow up and become responsible—quite the contrary. Games keep us stuck and emotionally immature. The choice is ours. Every choice, regardless of its nature, has a dilemma associated with it. If we continue to play games, we will remain emotionally immature, alienate people we care about, and frustrate those who try to help us. If we choose to grow up, it will be difficult. We will have to face many things about ourselves that we do not like. We will have to be honest with ourselves and others. We will need to feel emotions from which we have been running. But we will also know a personal freedom that is hard to imagine. The choice is ours.

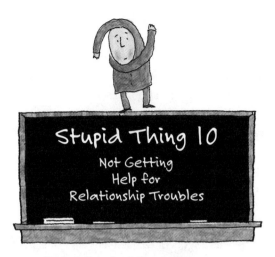

Stupid Thing 10
Not Getting Help for Relationship Troubles

Dysfunctional relationships are one
of the top three causes of relapse.

Here's a situation that recently presented itself to me in my practice. Walter and Carrie, two wonderful, attractive, young people, met and fell in love about two years ago. Walter had more than five years of recovery and Carrie was newly sober. Their life was filled with many promises, their values seemed similar, their goals compatible, and they enjoyed each other immensely. They soon married and began facing all of the challenges, pressures, and difficulties of married life. Complications arose from many directions, one of which involved Walter's child from a previous relationship. Carrie felt betrayed when Walter sought joint custody of his son, as this is not what she imagined would happen. Walter gave Carrie the impression that he would be only superficially involved with his son, that he was going to focus on building their life together and place a boundary between his present situation and his past. Financial concerns overrode his promise, and he felt compelled to seek custody because it made financial sense and because he was beginning to realize that he had a personal responsibility to his son. Walter believed that Carrie agreed with this idea because she didn't object. Yet he never really talked with her about his plan. That was a mistake.

Carrie resented Walter's idea, but she only objected indirectly. She swallowed her feelings and became resentful. What made matters even worse for this couple was that they had started down a path that would eventually destroy their relationship: they were letting fear and emotional dependency control their interactions. Demands erupted from both sides of the relationship. Carrie couldn't talk to any men at her AA meetings because Walter was threatened and felt jealous and insecure. On the other hand, Carrie wouldn't let Walter go to co-ed AA meetings because good-looking women were present and might hit on him. Slowly but surely they built a prison out of their love and commitment to each other. They couldn't do anything if it was going to cause one or the other to feel threatened or insecure. Love became the shackles that they firmly secured around each other's ankles.

As the restrictions increased, their love weakened. When we attempt to control our partner, love dies. Walter and Carrie both felt more and more controlled by their demands on each other, demands caused by their emotional dependency. Eventually, Carrie announced that she wanted a trial separation. She was no longer sure if she loved Walter. She was confused and uncertain whether being married was what she still wanted. Walter was devastated, and after almost eight years of sobriety, he wanted to take a drink and get loaded. He didn't know how to cope with such intense pain, loss, and anguish. Carrie was desperate. Their dreams had been shattered by the forces of emotional dependency. And now both were in danger of relapse.

Relationship problems are one of the top three reasons for relapse. Why? Because important relationships expose our emotional immaturity more than any other experience. The more a person means to us, the more trouble we have keeping ourselves centered and soothing ourselves when things are uncertain or when the person doesn't meet our expectations. When someone is very important to us, it is hard to hold on to ourselves when we feel disappointed, threatened, or frustrated.

As our partner's importance increases, our emotional dependency rears its ugly head and begins to influence our feelings and reactions. The more emotionally dependent we are, the more problematic and conflicted our relationship becomes. We begin to assert more and more pressure on our partner, both directly and indirectly, to take care of us—to make us feel good about ourselves, make us feel loved, make us feel alive, make us feel attractive or important, make us feel like a man or a woman, make us feel desirable, make us happy, and erase our emptiness or loneliness. When our partner doesn't behave according to our specifications, trouble starts and manifests itself in one of three ways: (1) we try to control our partner to ensure that he or she will do our bidding; (2) we submit to our partner's will; or (3) we run away by emotionally stonewalling our partner or literally splitting from the relationship.

All three of these maneuvers are based on emotional dependency. At times, these tactics provide a temporary solution to the pain, but the solution doesn't last because it is unstable. It's like building a house on a foundation of sand. It may have a great view and be solid enough when the conditions are moderate, but as soon as there is inclement weather, trouble begins.

Any relationship that requires our partner to behave a certain way in order for us to feel okay or good about ourselves will not work in the long run. Eventually something will happen and our partner will not meet our specifications or demands. For whatever reason, our partner will be unable to be there for us in the manner that we have come to expect. How we react to this disappointment will help us identify the strength of our emotional dependency: the stronger our emotional dependency, the stronger our reaction to disappointment.

We need to identify and deal with our emotional immaturity and how it is controlling us, or the relationship will not survive. This is when a relapse is most likely to occur. Many times I have seen people in recovery relapse when their relationship hits the wall. But there is a solution to relationship problems if we develop the following perspective.

Consider responding to relationship difficulties with "of course." I discuss this strategy in my book *Love Secrets Revealed*. *Of course* there is going to be trouble in your relationship because your partner is important to you. Relationship problems don't indicate that something is wrong; quite the opposite is true. Problems indicate that something is right; we pick a partner who will cause a particular kind of trouble in our life. The trouble we encounter gives us an opportunity to take the next step in our emotional and spiritual development. Problems are gifts that need to be carefully unwrapped. If we put our problems into a healthy perspective, we will be well on the way to discovering a real solution.

We are all ignorant when it comes to knowing how to make a relationship work. We just don't know what we don't know, and our emotional immaturity compounds the situation because we won't ask for help. This is why I am suggesting that our first response be "of course." So what do we do when we are in trouble and we don't know what to do about it? We need to ask for help.

The dynamics inherent in relationships are complex and challenging and have the potential to bring out our best or our worst behavior. This is why there is much truth in the saying "We save our worst behaviors for those we love and care about." The fact that we typically treat strangers better than those we love is a painful reality. When we finally surrender and accept that relationships are difficult, we can get on with growing up and facing our ignorance instead of complaining about our partners or running away from them.

Some of you may ruffle when I diagnose this problem as ignorance. For me, ignorance is the most appropriate diagnosis for the cause of our troubles because it offers hope. Ignorance can be corrected with new information. New information is necessary because we can only do what we know how to do, which we realize is not enough. We must be open to help because it is hard to see how emotional dependency is affecting the climate of our relationships when we are so close to the problem. The program works by being honest, open, and willing.

Many of us lose sight of the fact that we are part of our relationship problems. We may waste time by focusing on our partner's behavior, when focusing on our behavior is much more helpful. If we can't see our part, we can ask our partner—if we're open to what our partner might say. If we're not, we can ask a friend or sponsor to give feedback. If that person's feedback proves insufficient, we can turn to a qualified professional therapist who specializes in relationships and recovery.

This is the kind of rigorous honesty that will help us establish true emotional sobriety in our recovery. Emotional sobriety eludes many people who fill the rooms in AA, NA, and the like. Earnie Larsen, author and lecturer, called this *Stage II recovery.* Stage II recovery is concerned with learning how to have healthy relationships, and we can't have a healthy relationship if we are emotionally fused with our partner. Chronic emotional dependency will eventually destroy all of the good in the relationship. There is hope, but it takes a commitment, an open mind, new information, and a good therapist or coach to help. There is nothing like the challenges that come from a relationship to help us take the next step in recovery.

In summary, we are sabotaging our recovery if we are having

trouble in our relationship and we refuse to get help. Trust me when I say that the relationship problems will persist; they will not magically disappear until we address their source. If we are painstaking about this phase of our development, we will discover that emotional dependency is a real problem in our life. Until we face how we are emotionally dependent and how it affects our self-esteem, self-worth, and self-confidence, real emotional sobriety will elude us and we will be more likely to relapse.

Those who have open-heartedly started the process of growing up are rewarded with emotional sobriety. Emotional sobriety is the next step in our recovery and is achieved by balancing our desire to please and our desire to be ourselves. We achieve this by eradicating our absolute dependency on people, places, and things. Wow, what an order! Do not be discouraged. I have seen many long-timers who, having grown up and faced their emotional immaturity, are now enjoying a serenity and peace of mind that they would have never dreamed possible. They are men and women like us who were once ignorant, immature, and emotionally dependent. There is hope!

Stupid Thing 11
Believing That Life Should Be Easy

Life is difficult. The sooner we are initiated into this reality, the sooner we learn how to deal with life on its terms rather than waste our time looking for the easy way.

The myth that life should be easy is ubiquitous in our culture. We are obsessed with it. We spend billions of dollars on weight-loss programs and wonder drugs. In homes across the United States, exercise equipment that promised a body like Arnold Schwarzenegger's in just fifteen minutes a day is gathering dust in a corner. We flock to weekend growth groups and retreats, hoping that we will change our life in two weekends. We participate in multilevel marketing schemes that insist we will be able to earn a million dollars in just one year, or we buy into real estate schemes that promise earning potential with no money down. We subject ourselves to plastic surgery to give us the shape we desire without ever having to set foot in a gym. Or we undergo liposuction to remove unwanted fat without having to modify our diet and eat sensibly. We purchase energy drinks and coffee to provide us with the lift we need, which gives us enthusiasm for what we are doing because it's not what we want to be doing in the first place. We allow ourselves to be anesthetized for twenty-four hours while the doctor administers intolerable levels of naltrexone to facilitate detoxification. We are a nation obsessed with finding the easiest solution. Where are we heading with such madness?

The idea that life should be easy is one of the myths or attitudes that set us up for addiction. Our obsession with this notion is fertile ground for us to turn toward alcohol and other drugs for a quick fix to our pain, regardless of whether it is caused by depression, anxiety, fear, insecurities, stress, relationship problems, low self-esteem, an abusive relationship, or childhood trauma. Dealing with painful experiences and anxiety is not easy, and we are setting ourselves up if we expect it to be easy. I have seen many patients drop out of therapy or stop attending meetings because things got worse before they got better.

The truth is that this is exactly what is supposed to happen. As we begin to get more honest with ourselves, we see things that we don't like about ourselves and confront things that we have been hiding from ourselves. Growing up requires the ability to support ourselves in our growth with an unfailing commitment. Most people are unwilling to make this kind of a commitment unless their backs are up against the wall.

A culture based on the easy way is doomed to fail. It cultivates neither wisdom nor spirituality and perpetuates emotional immaturity. Finding the easy way is an infantile wish that often persists into adulthood. This curse permeates every level of our society, and yet we buy into it wholeheartedly. The results are reflected in our personal behavior and in the state of our institutions: a husband gets enraged because his wife won't give in to his emotional blackmail; an employee demands a raise even though the quality of his work doesn't warrant such recognition; an institution of higher education drops the requirement of mastering a second language from their doctoral programs because it is too hard; a school drops its grading standards to make it easier for children to get good grades; an athletic program deemphasizes competition to ensure that all kids will play; when a teacher is being hard on a child, the parents protect their child instead of working with their child to address the problems. Many people in recovery don't work the Fourth Step because "it's too hard."

How to counter this cultural conspiracy to keep us emotionally immature is an important issue for each of us to face. Some cultures have avoided the problem altogether. Initiation rites are an experiential process used in some cultures to create a personal transformation, such as a rite of passage from boyhood to manhood. The initiation process is designed to achieve three things. First, the process is purgative. The experience facilitates a purging, or surrendering, of the boyhood ego and creates a deep sense of humility. Humility is the foundation for this personal transformation. Second, the process is illuminative. It helps the young man see life from a new perspective by interacting with other initiated men or wise elders; it opens him to a larger reality than his small, egocentric world. The young man learns that life is not about him, that there is a much larger purpose to his life. And third, the process is uniting and integrative. It helps the participant return to the community transformed into a man who can contribute to society. The participant is transformed into a new, spiritual person and is welcomed back into the community.

A rite of passage teaches the important truth that life is difficult. The young man is hazed, scared, frightened, and he faces ordeals that push him to the brink of his physical and mental abilities. He is broken down mentally and physically. He may be cut and bleed, symbolic of how hard life is. The scars left by these wounds are meant to be constant reminders of this important lesson. The young man understands, surrenders to, and accepts the results of the ordeal.

Life is difficult and he knows it, without ever having read M. Scott Peck's wonderful book *The Road Less Traveled*.

If we accept that this is life's baseline, then we are not seduced by the idea that all our days will be good ones and that the easiest path is something one should expect. We accept good days for what they are. We accept difficult days in the same spirit. We do not look for the quick or easy fix; we take life as it is rather than trying to turn it into something it is not. We don't fight life or complain about our lot—we accept life on its terms, not ours. Isn't this the message from most spiritual teachers?

The resistance to using this solution in life is that acceptance is not embraced in our society. It is too passive, which is not valued in our society. We are a "can do" nation. Our nation's motto seems to be "We can do or achieve anything we want if we just put our mind to it." This is a partial truth, not the whole truth. The remainder of the truth is that we need to learn how to accept the things we cannot change as well as act on the things we can. Sorting out these differences is a challenge and requires wisdom gained from life experiences. This is the powerful message behind the Serenity Prayer: "God, grant me the serenity to accept the things I cannot change, the courage to change the things I can, and the wisdom to know the difference." Discerning whether action or acceptance is the best response is a hallmark of wisdom. When we correctly assess a situation and respond appropriately, we are in sync with life; we are not at cross-purposes. When we inaccurately assess a situation and try to force a change or control the outcome, we create tension and struggle. This type of struggle contaminates the emotional climate of our entire life.

Serenity is achieved through being in sync with life, but don't expect to be in sync often. Research has demonstrated that we are not in sync with life more than one third of the time. Yet we expect that we should be most of the time, and when our expectations do not fit, we get mad, depressed, or withdrawn. Instead of meeting these situations with the "of course" response we learned about in the last chapter, we try to force our loved ones, our employer or employees, even life itself to live up to our expectations, and when they don't, we feel defeated. We take their responses personally and we are off to visit Miseryville, which lies just south of Self-Loathing Hills.

When we accept life for what it is, we will see tremendous benefits. We stop judging. Judgment is irrelevant because life is what it is. We don't need to control or change our partner, our life, or our friends. We accept them the way they are, and if we don't like it, then we dig into the meaning of our reaction instead of trying to make others feel bad about who they are. Once we stop manipulating people, places, and things, we free up all of that energy and put it to work on our own personal development, which is where it is best focused in the first place.

Stupid Thing 12
Using the Program to Handle Everything

No one can handle every personal issue with their program. Needing help is not an indication that something is wrong with our program. The truth is quite the contrary: recognizing our need for additional help is an indication that we are working a good program.

Harry Tiebout, M.D., a psychiatrist who was befriended by AA shortly after its conception, described what he called "a defiant self-reliance" in the personalities of the alcoholics he treated. I, too, have seen this in my clinical experience. I think of it as an overdetermined independence; we don't want to need anyone. We despise dependency, and we therefore deny any part of our selves or our life that isn't totally self-sufficient. This defiant independence creates an over-reliance on self. We rely exclusively on ourselves for solutions, and most of the time, this presents a serious problem.

Remember the discussion on pages 18–19 regarding the neuro-psychological effects of drug use, including alcohol, on the brain? Two brain functions are impaired: abstract thinking and problem-solving abilities. Both of these cognitive functions are necessary to effectively cope with life. If we are unable to use our abstract thinking, we can't see the big picture. We end up focusing on irrelevant issues because our perspective of the problem is narrow; we ultimately miss critical information. To make matters even worse, we selectively perceive only those things that are congruent with our current beliefs and behavior. This means that we are unable to successfully gather information from our experiences, and we form misleading conclusions. We conclude that something isn't a problem when it is or that something is a problem when it isn't. This is what happens when reluctant newcomers attend a meeting and focus on how different they are from the AA speaker instead of how similar they are. They falsely conclude that they don't have a problem because they aren't like the speaker.

When our ability to problem solve is impaired, we are stuck in what is called a *sincere delusion.* We sincerely believe that we don't have a problem when in fact we do. We don't want to see a problem because we are too invested in not having a problem. So we end up blaming others or generating endless justifications for our rotten behavior. I used to have trouble believing that sincere delusion existed, but I have grown to accept this assessment as accurate. We abhor helplessness, and therefore, our minds do not let us see that which we cannot fix. So we deceive ourselves into thinking, *It's not as much of a problem as everyone is making it out to be.* We need to be suspicious of our ideas; they are clearly biased and limited by our perception.

So here is the ongoing dilemma. A part of each of us wants to do it alone; our false pride dictates self-reliance. At the same time, we are lost and unable to discover a solution to our problems. Here's the tough pill to swallow: we are ignorant and don't want to admit it. We all struggle with a number of different issues. For instance, some of us don't know how to stay sober, or deal with disappointment, or cope with difficulties in our relationships. Some of us may be stuck on the Fourth Step and don't know how to unblock ourselves from the resistance we feel whenever we sit down to write our personal inventory. Some of us may be struggling with personality conflicts at work. Or some may be in love and not know how to tell that person about our feelings.

One thing is for certain: if we continue to honor our false pride, it will hamper and ultimately sabotage our recovery. Recovery is the antithesis of the disease. While using, we ignored our limitations and were unable to ask for help. In recovery, we do the opposite. We acknowledge and respect our limitations and identify our blind spots, rather than ignore and deny them.

For this and many other reasons, it is crucial to find a sponsor! A sponsor is our personal guide to working the Twelve Steps. If we don't yet have a sponsor, we may wonder, *How am I going to find the right person?* I have heard many newly clean-and-sober patients anguish over this decision.

Here's my advice. Pick a person of the same sex who has successfully and rigorously worked all Twelve Steps. Choose someone who works a program that attracts you, a person who deals with feelings in the way that you think would be healthy for you too; a person who holds on to his or her individuality and at the same time cooperates with others; a person who has a personal relationship with a God of his or her understanding; a person who walks the talk; a person with integrity and humility but who is also appropriately assertive. Select a person who has what you want.

If you are newly sober, you might feel silly about asking a person to sponsor you. You may not feel worthy of asking someone for help, as if you don't deserve his or her time. Others have mentioned that they fear being rejected. I understand these feelings. I really do. What you don't yet realize is that sponsorship is as important for the sponsor as it is for the sponsee. Being of value to another suffering alcoholic or addict helps the sponsor stay sober as much as it helps the newcomer. The relationship is quid pro quo—something is given as well as received. So don't hesitate to ask someone to sponsor you. Most Twelve Step members feel honored to help newcomers.

If you find enough courage to ask a person to sponsor you and that person says no, don't take it personally. That response tells you something about him or her and says nothing about you. There may be a variety of reasons why the person declines your request. Check it out. Most of the time you will be surprised to learn that the decision has nothing to do with you.

It's amazing how important we think we are. We are not that important. In Al-Anon we hear it said, "It's not what they're doing to you, it's just what they are doing." Keep trying. Plenty of members are eager to sponsor newcomers. In some meetings, there is a show of hands of people who are willing to sponsor.

Once you have found a sponsor, the next step is to establish a personal relationship with him or her. Spend as much time with your sponsor as possible. Read program literature together, discuss readings, work the Steps together, share your personal dilemmas, hopes, dreams, and frustrations. Welcome this person into your inner circle. Offer to accompany your sponsor on Twelve Step calls and try to be of assistance in whatever manner possible. This is the best way to establish rapport, which is essential in the sponsor-sponsee relationship. Your sponsor has much to teach you. A sponsor is the mentor, and you are the apprentice. Instead of learning a trade or an occupational skill, you are learning life skills for how to live clean and sober. You are learning how to work the Twelve Steps and practice spiritual principles in all your affairs. You are learning how to function as a clean-and-sober person. This is what happens in recovery. You learn how to get clean, then you learn how to stay clean, and finally you learn how to live clean. The last stage of recovery—learning how to live clean and sober—is a lifelong process. Your sponsor can be valuable at every one of these stages of recovery, but only if you are open and honest.

If you already have a sponsor and you are not investing yourself in that relationship, you are playing the "I have a sponsor" game. The purpose of this game is to create the image that you are working the program when you are not; you are just doing what you are "supposed" to do. If this is true, then you are sabotaging your recovery.

Another way people sabotage their relationship with their sponsor is by being *selectively* honest. They only share *partial* truths about what is happening in their lives and typically leave out crucial information. False pride filters out the information we are ashamed of, and we fear being judged and criticized. A sponsor's reaction is not the problem. The problem is our own self-hate. Most people do not judge us as harshly as we judge ourselves. So take a risk. Share something risky. Potential freedom is worth the risk that you take.

Blind spots and false pride sabotage the quality of recovery. A man I treated twenty years ago was very abusive to his wife. He would berate her when he became frustrated, denigrate her, call her names, and terrorize her when she did not do what he wanted her to do. In our first session, I challenged him about his abusive behavior and he justified his behavior by hiding behind rationalizations like "Sometimes a man has to stand up for himself" or "I won't take her controlling behavior any longer." While she was no angel, he couldn't see that he wasn't either. What I was trying to help him see was how his response was a part of the problem, not a part of the solution. What she was doing was her problem, and what he was doing was his. But he used her behavior to justify his rotten behavior. He played tit-for-tat and used it to justify his arrogant and vindictive response. This part of him couldn't have a healthy relationship; he wanted to win, be right, control her, get even, and have power over her. His perceptions and interpretations of her behavior were projections of his own controlling and vindictive impulses. That's why he reacted so negatively to her. Every time he would go off on a diatribe about her undesirable behavior, he was really talking about himself. He couldn't see what he was doing because he didn't want to—he would then have to face his vindictive and controlling ways. This conflicted with his self-image. His cruel and hurtful behavior didn't fit his idea of himself as a clean-and-sober person with long-term recovery.

His self-deception interfered with his AA program and ultimately his relationship with his sponsor. He presented himself at AA meetings as if he were working a great program. His AA pitch was impressive, and he sounded like he was well on the road to recovery. The problem was that he was not being honest about how he really functioned in his relationship; he did not want to see the truth about his abusive behavior so he compartmentalized and projected it. He blocked out any awareness of his abusiveness in order to deceive himself into believing he was healthier than he really was. He played all kinds of games with himself in order to avoid facing the truth: he was a bully and didn't know how to really respect and honor another person's feelings. He never learned from his parents how to respect others and he was repeating the same curse that he was subjected to as a child. His upbringing wasn't his fault, but he was and is responsible and accountable for what he does today. He is no longer a child.

When he would meet with his sponsor, which he did often because it reinforced the image of a hard-working AA member, he would omit any reference to how he was really behaving. Instead, he painted a distorted picture to look righteous. His sponsor had no idea of what was really going on and therefore couldn't really help. Eventually this man lost his wife and custody of his four children because he was unable to be honest with himself and open up to his sponsor. He couldn't support himself enough to be open and vulnerable. In his mind, vulnerability was weak and humiliating and therefore not an option. This was a real pity because his sponsor was a good man and could have been quite helpful.

This story does not have a happy ending; it never does when we let false pride run our life. This man now lives a very bitter and angry life, blaming everyone for his problems: his vindictive wife, his exploitive employer, his ungrateful children, the jealous or threatened AA members, the bad drivers where he lives, and the therapist who sided with his wife. This man sabotaged his recovery by not being honest with himself and his sponsor. He was more concerned with saving face than with saving his life. His need to see himself in a glorified light was so strong that he deceived himself into believing his own distortions.

We don't have to stay stuck in unhealthy behavior. There is hope. A qualified therapist or counselor can be just the thing we need to move to the next level in our recovery. Moving forward, whether with a sponsor or a therapist, requires honesty. There are many times when seeking outside help is necessary, for example, for severe and incapacitating depression or anxiety, chronic relationship problems, underachievement, childhood traumas that interfere with daily functioning, sexual dysfunction, insomnia, uncontrollable anger and rage, self-hate, sexual addiction, crippling fear of social interactions, inability to support ourselves in the pursuit of our dreams, relationship failures at work, persistent thoughts of suicide, feeling lost and alone, thinking of drinking or using all the time, self-mutilation, and simply not being happy with our life.

From my point of view, the only legitimate reason not to seek outside help is if we're hoping that therapy will be easier and softer than a Twelve Step program. If we use therapy to avoid working the program, then we are using therapy to help sabotage recovery.

If you believe you need to see a therapist, talk about it with your sponsor and express your hopes and concerns. If your sponsor is against therapy, find out why. Explore your sponsor's objection. If you are uncomfortable with your sponsor's recommendation, then raise the issue in a closed meeting where you can get some feedback from other program members. You are not being disloyal to your sponsor. Inform him or her of your intention to get additional feedback on this issue. Remember your sponsor is only human, and he or she may suffer from a personal bias.

While one of the Traditions of AA states that AA has no opinion on outside issues, it doesn't mean that all members honor this principle. Some program members are critical of those who seek outside help from a therapist. Sometimes these critics have had negative, maybe even harmful, experiences with a psychiatrist or therapist and therefore lump all therapists in the same category of "avoid at all costs." Others are just ignorant and stereotype all mental health professionals as incompetent.

If you are thinking about getting outside help, become an informed consumer. Not all therapists are created equal. Some therapists will be a better fit for you than others. I recommend you interview the person you are considering by scheduling an appointment. Inform the therapist that you'd like a trial session to determine whether you are compatible. Encourage the therapist to conduct an actual session where you discuss an important issue in your life and the therapist works with you on it. This gives you firsthand knowledge of what it would be like to work with this person. Pay attention to your reaction. Was the session helpful? Were you challenged to look at your behavior or the situation in a different way? Did you leave with some new information or self-knowledge? Did you feel understood by and connected with the therapist?

Don't expect yourself to like what your therapist tells you, because sometimes you won't. There are going to be times in therapy when your therapist confronts you and you won't like it. So expect yourself to feel challenged in a helpful and useful manner. A therapeutic confrontation will cause you to reach further than you typically do and explore areas that you have not looked at. Use all of this information to make a decision about whom you will work with.

While it is not always necessary for your therapist to have knowledge of recovery and addiction, it is often very helpful. A solid therapist could be helpful regardless of his or her knowledge of Twelve Step programs. However, a therapist who has experience with recovery and addiction may be able to help you spot ways that you are sabotaging your recovery.

Remember that you are the consumer. The therapist is working to help you function better in your life; he or she is there for your best interest. And you get to decide what is in your best interest. It is your life! While the therapist is responsible for the therapy, you are ultimately responsible for your life.

If you are uncomfortable with your therapist or believe he or she is not that helpful, then talk this over with him or her. Share your discomfort, concerns, and expectations; see whether you and your therapist can work through these issues and feelings. If, for whatever reason, your therapist is not right for you and you have explored your concerns with your therapist, it may be time to move on and find a better match. I tell each of my new patients that they need to decide whether I am right for them. Penicillin can save one person's life, but it can kill the next person if he or she is allergic to the drug.

As I said earlier in this chapter, defiant self-reliance and our pride system protects a false self-image that ultimately stops us from seeking help when we need it. Keep an eye out for this dynamic. If our false pride is running the show, it is sabotaging our recovery in one way or another. Drinking is only one way that we sabotage our recovery. There are many subtle ways in which we prevent ourselves from enjoying all of the benefits of recovery. The choice is ours. Do we continue to let our false pride dictate what is and isn't right? Or do we turn to a higher self within us that is seeking a spiritual solution to our dilemmas? These are very different paths, each containing their own challenges, pitfalls, and rewards. Never forget that we suffer from a medical illness that has a spiritual solution. A fit spiritual condition is our only hope of arresting alcoholism and other drug addictions. There is no mental defense against addiction; we either have a spiritual connection or we don't.

Some Final Thoughts and Suggestions

In this book I have discussed twelve ways that many well-intentioned people sabotage their recovery. There are as many ways to sabotage recovery as there are people in recovery. Instead of trying to create an exhaustive list, I have presented what I see as the most common hazards encountered during the first two years of recovery. If you have identified these thoughts, ideas, or behaviors in your life, then do yourself a favor and start talking about it in your meetings, with your sponsor, or with your therapist. You don't have to continue down a self-destructive path. There is hope, but only if you act and change your attitude. Get off your back and on your side!

In the introduction, I identified the four culprits lurking in the shadows of your self-destructive behavior:

1. your addiction, or your disease
2. ignorance
3. unreasonable expectations and emotional dependency
4. self-erasure and self-hate

The rest of this book offers suggestions for how to address these issues so that they are no longer lurking in the shadows, waiting to pounce on you and sabotage your recovery.

Your Addiction, or Your Disease

If you have identified this as the factor in your self-destructive behavior, consider yourself in danger. Imagine you are sitting in my office and I am jumping up and down in front of you like a madman, desperately waving a large red flag, warning you of danger.

You are at risk because once again your disease is taking control of your life. If you don't do something immediately to reverse this process, you will eventually return to drinking or using other drugs. You need help! The solution for arresting your disease lies in working the Twelve Steps. I consider the Twelve Steps *disease busters.* They provide the only reliable antidote for this terrible illness. Some people have found other useful ways to deal with addiction, but the Twelve Steps are unparalleled in their success at helping people become free from addiction. The Twelve Steps are the best-known solution to alcoholism and other addictions.

Many times you can find the flaw in your recovery by reviewing your Twelve Step work. For instance, many individuals who are chronically relapsing discover that they have not completely surrendered to the reality of their condition: their total and utter powerlessness over alcohol or other drugs and the unmanageability of their lives. Until you surrender 100 percent, you will not be able to build a successful foundation for your recovery.

I hope you are now asking yourself, *Okay Doc, I know that I have not surrendered, but I don't know what to do about it. Do you have any suggestions?* I am glad you asked because I do have some thoughts about what you can do and an exercise for you to try.

You need to address why you can't accept the fact that you are powerless over alcohol and other drugs. Until you can identify and address how you are preventing yourself from surrendering, you will be stuck in an endless loop of trying to get clean and then relapsing. So let's explore what may be blocking you, where you are resisting this reality. I can give you many ideas of what might be interfering with your surrender, but I would prefer it if you tried to discover it on your own.

A therapeutic exercise that I often do with my patients is to have them respond to incomplete sentences with the first thought that comes to their minds. So here is what I would like you to do. I am going to present you with a list of incomplete sentences. I want you to get a notebook and a pen. Next I want you to write down one incomplete sentence on the top of each page. Respond to each incomplete sentence with as many endings as come to mind. Be aware of your reaction to each sentence and write it down. For instance, if I ask you to respond to "The most difficult thing about admitting that I am powerless over alcohol and other drugs is . . ." and you thought, *I don't want to know the answer to that question,* then write that down first. Keep going, silently asking yourself the question again and writing down your next response. Continue until you have written down all your responses. Remember, whatever comes to your mind is grist for the therapeutic mill.

As you do this exercise, resist the desire to judge what you are thinking. Instead, observe your reaction and write it down exactly as you think it. There will come a time for you to look at what it all means later. For now, just become aware of how you are blocking yourself from admitting and surrendering to your powerlessness over alcohol and other drugs. So here we go. Write down your responses to the following incomplete sentences:

- My addiction is planning to defeat all my recovery efforts by . . .
- The addict in me is planning to . . .
- When I imagine a life without using, I feel . . .
- A scary thing about recovery is . . .
- A scary thing about using again is . . .
- Using was my way of trying to say . . .
- It's very hard for me to face . . .
- One thing that the addict in me doesn't want to admit is . . .
- If the addict in me could speak to you, he or she would say . . .
- A clean-and-sober life might offer me hope for . . .
- What my addiction doesn't want you to know is . . .
- What surrender means to me is . . .
- If I admit I am powerless over alcohol and other drugs, it would mean . . .
- If I admit I am powerless over alcohol and other drugs, my opinion about myself would be . . .
- A way I fool myself into thinking that I am not powerless over alcohol and other drugs is . . .
- If I made a list of the events that indicate that I am powerless over alcohol and other drugs, I would have to conclude . . .
- I am ashamed of . . .

Now read your answers out loud to yourself. Often when you read out loud something you have written, you hear it differently than when you were writing. Ask yourself the following questions:

- Can I identify patterns or themes to my responses?
- Am I able to put my finger on what I am doing to interfere with my surrender?
- What am I aware of as I review my responses?

Share your answers with your sponsor or your therapist. I recommend that you read them out loud to him or her too. Ask your sponsor the three questions that I posed to you. Get his or her feedback. Sometimes awareness itself starts the process of change.

I hope this exercise will help you identify how you block your surrender. The next thing I would like you to do is to share your dilemma in meetings. Whenever a request is made in a meeting for a topic, ask the group to discuss surrender and the difficulties experienced in surrendering. When you have an opportunity, discuss your difficulty and ask the group members to share their experiences, strengths, and hopes with you. This open discussion of your dilemma and the awareness-enhancing exercise may help you embrace and surrender to the reality of your powerlessness.

Ignorance

The second issue in diagnosing the cause of your self-defeating or self-destructive behavior is ignorance. You don't know what you don't know. If you identify this as the cause of your problems, the cure is obvious: acquire information. But if you are too ashamed to let your sponsor, therapist, or fellow program members know that you don't know, you will never acquire the information you so desperately need. I love what my editor's fifth-grade teacher once said, "Better to be a fool for five minutes than forever."

I believe shame is a product of false pride. Shame is created when we believe we are not living up to our image of an idealized person. When we fall short of this concept, we begin to despise ourselves; shame (a close cousin of self-hate) results. Some of us may be thinking that self-hate is too strong of a label. Believe me, it's not. We just don't let ourselves see our self-hate. We defend against it by blocking it out of awareness. However, if we look close, we can glimpse our self-hate when it spikes in our life, especially when we do something that we judge as ridiculous or stupid or not how we think we should be. When we behave in one of these ways, we feel the real strength and pervasiveness of our self-hate.

We develop a pride system to support our idealized image. Our pride system ensures that we are going to act according to the set of standards generated by our idealized image. These become the *shoulds* that run our life. We become tyrannized by these standards, whether they are reasonable or not. False pride is a system we develop to ensure our adherence to these standards.

Poke around in your psyche and see if your false pride is interfering with your education. By becoming aware of how your false pride is impeding your growth, you can begin to dismantle this self-constructed barrier to recovery. It is not a crime to be ignorant. Once you become aware of how your false pride is blocking your ability to learn, you will then have the choice to rescind its privilege.

An exercise that may be helpful is to make a list of your *shoulds*. On the top of a piece of paper write "I should . . ." and then write all of the responses that come to mind. You will be blown away at how many *shoulds* you can come up with. No wonder we are so messed up. How can we ever find out who we really are under such an onslaught of impossible demands and unreasonable standards?

Another tool that may be useful in dismantling your false self is to use the traditional Fourth Step inventory presented in the Big Book of AA. If you conduct an inventory of your false pride with your sponsor, you will discover how limiting and destructive it truly is.

I want to encourage you to be rigorously honest with yourself when you do this work, because it is only with rigorous honesty that you will begin to find a solution to your problems. If working on this issue with your sponsor isn't enough, find a qualified therapist. Meet with the therapist you have selected and explore this issue. See how the therapist works with you, how he or she guides you to examine your false pride, and how he or she works with it. If you begin understanding and dismantling your false pride, then you know you have found the right therapist.

Unreasonable Expectations and Emotional Dependency

I believe that we are all unreasonable in our expectations of ourselves and others. The unreasonable claims we make are serious problems in recovery because they form the basis for resentments. Resentments are deadly and often play a major role in relapse. Not resolving your resentments is a sure way of sabotaging your recovery.

Increasing self-awareness is the first step toward dealing with unreasonable expectations. Because we have the ability to deceive ourselves into thinking that we are reasonable and that it is everyone else who is unreasonable, we are often unaware of how truly outrageous we are.

Give yourself permission to go beyond being reasonable. Exaggerate being unreasonable. Give yourself permission to answer the following questions as outrageously and unreasonably as you can muster. Don't hold back. Be bold and absurd and have some fun.

- If I really told you what I want from you, I would ask for . . .
- If I really let myself be outrageous, I would . . .
- I demand that you . . .
- What I secretly feel about myself is . . .
- I expect myself to be . . .
- Recovery should be . . .
- If I were honest with you about my expectations, I would tell you . . .
- The most disappointing thing about recovery is . . .
- The most exciting thing about recovery is . . .

Once you have written at least five responses to each of these sentences, share them with someone you trust. Search for the underlying claim in your responses. You may be surprised at what turns up. Hint: Emotional dependency is likely to be evident somewhere in your responses.

One of the most powerful moments in my recovery came when I realized that two problems underlying my expectations were perfectionism and emotional dependency. My expectations were based on demands and specifications that I imposed on people, places, and things regarding how they were supposed to act and how life was supposed to be. Through much work in the program and countless hours of therapy, I am learning how to hold on to myself rather than control or manipulate others. I am trying to accept life as it is, rather than impose my demands and expectations on it. So, if your life or relationships aren't working out according to your beliefs, dig into your psyche and see whether you can identify any of the issues discussed in this section.

Others in recovery who struggle with anxiety or depression, like Bill Wilson, discover that they have not dealt with their emotional dependency. They are still trying to find perfect romance, perfect security, or perfect success, believing that once they acquire these things, they will be all right. Wrong! *It is not what you have that will make you all right, it is who you are.* It is how we deal with our feelings, our relationships, and feelings toward ourselves that will make us feel comfortable in our own skin. The bottom line is that we need to learn how to take care of ourselves instead of manipulating others to take care of us. Most of us are much more skilled at manipulating others to get what we need than we are at acting on our own behalf and taking responsibility for our own personal desires. But this doesn't mean that we aren't able to learn how to take care of ourselves. We can, with a little help from our friends and a qualified therapist when necessary.

Self-Erasure and Self-Hate

The cure for self-erasure and self-hate is based on complete and total reconciliation with ourselves. Self-compassion cures self-hate. When we develop a compassionate attitude toward ourselves, we begin to reverse the effects of self-hate. Many people confuse self-compassion for selfishness or self-indulgence. But it is neither. In *Compassion and Self-Hate,* Theodore Isaac Rubin's definition is quite helpful in gaining a thorough understanding of this concept:

> Self-compassion is any thoughts, feelings, moods, insights, and actions that serve the best interest of the actual self. This includes all functions which protect, sustain, and enhance the actual self, all functions that diminish and destroy self-hate, and all functions that increase self-acceptance.

Recovery clearly is an act of self-compassion. The process that helps us stay clean and sober helps us recover our true self. When we work the Steps, we shatter our false self and begin to make progress in finding our true self. We reconnect with an important part of ourselves that we lost.

When we set boundaries with our parents, partners, co-workers, employers, strangers, siblings, or anyone else, we are honoring our true self. When we identify and challenge our self-hate, we are serving the best interest of our true self. When we reach out for help or reach out to a therapist, we are acting in the best interest of our true self. When we work the Twelve Steps, we are working in the best interest of our true self. When we challenge and block our unreasonable expectations, we are serving the best interest of our true self. When we face our emotional dependency, begin standing on our own two feet, and become self-supportive, we are serving the best interest of our true self.

Dr. Rubin recommends a four-step process in dealing with self-hate:

1. become aware of self-hate in its direct and indirect manifestations
2. surrender our special status that feeds our self-hate
3. block or challenge our self-hate
4. replace self-hate with self-compassion

As I have emphasized over and over again, change begins with awareness. Here are some incomplete sentences I suggest you complete:

- I show my hate for myself by . . .
- I am disappointed with myself for . . .
- I wish I never . . .
- What would make me like myself more would be . . .
- If I stopped hating myself, I would be able to . . .
- I sometimes wonder what my life would be like if I . . .
- I can never forgive myself for . . .

Once we have identified our self-hate, the next step in Dr. Rubin's process is to surrender our special status. This confuses most of my clients; they aren't sure what this means. *Special status* refers to a particular attitude we have toward ourselves, such as expecting ourselves to be perfect. Surrendering our special status means that we give up the idea that we can be perfect; we let go of the idea that we will ever be perfect; and we begin to strive for something more realistic, like progress rather than perfection.

Take John, for instance. In dealing with his self-hate, he realized that he hated himself for being needy. He grew up with the idea that a man should be needless and wantless. Therefore, any need or personal desire he experienced was either denied or projected on to others. He was ashamed of these feelings and, therefore, went to great lengths to deny them. In his recovery, he realized that it was human to have needs and personal desires. He had to surrender his special status to have a more compassionate relationship with himself.

Special status also relates to expectations regarding how others should treat you. I remember the powerful awakening I had when I realized that I wanted other people to honor my feelings more than I honored them myself. This was most obvious in my first marriage. I always knew I wanted to have children. I had an incredible relationship with my father and had a deep desire to be a father too. But when I married my first wife, Denise, I neither expressed my feelings about parenthood nor checked out how she felt about parenthood. I was in love, and I believed love would solve all our problems. It didn't!

Our love was very deep and sincere, but our differences regarding parenthood were a real problem. She wasn't at all interested in having children. She wanted a career and personal freedom, and children didn't fit into the picture for her. As I look back on this situation today, I believe that at some level I sensed her position on parenthood, but I didn't want to face it because it would mean the end of our marriage. I didn't want to leave her. I loved her deeply, and I also wanted to be a dad. We talked about adoption, but she didn't want children. It wasn't just childbearing that she objected to, it was being a mom in any shape or form.

I tried to manipulate her into giving me what I wanted. I pressured her to honor my feelings. I argued that having children was the "normal" thing to do, implying that she wasn't a normal woman because of her position. What a louse I was to lay that kind of a trip on her. Not once did I consider what would have happened had she caved in to my pressure. I was blinded by selfishness. Would I really want to have a child with a woman who didn't want to be a mother? Of course not, but I was too immature to consider this at the time.

I was furious with her for not giving me what I wanted. This is how my special status manifested itself. I wanted Denise to honor my desires more than I was willing to honor my own, and even more than I was willing to honor her feelings.

I did not want to walk away from the marriage, and I didn't want to face the pain and anxiety that this would cause me on several levels. I was a coward, and I didn't want to face that either. Surrendering my special status, which demanded that if she loved me she would sacrifice her feelings to make me happy, was an important step in growing up and moving beyond self-hate. When Denise didn't respond to my unreasonable demands, I either criticized or showed contempt for her. I also turned it around and hated myself for not being enough or more of a man, lover, partner—falsely concluding that this was why she wouldn't honor my feelings. I took the proverbial dirty shoe off one foot and put it on the other, instead of cleaning the dirt off the shoe.

This was just one of the outrageous demands and ridiculous claims that I have placed on myself and others. There are numerous others, which I continue to realize and challenge on a regular basis. What has helped tremendously in gaining and maintaining a healthy perspective is reminding myself that, as page 58 of the Big Book says, "Some of us have tried to hold on to our old ideas and the result was nil until we let go absolutely." There are many old ideas with which I struggle, which is one of the reasons why recovery is an ongoing process.

The next step in this process is to block or challenge self-hate. In order to do this, we must be able to recognize the voice of self-hate. I hope the exercise you did on page 108 has facilitated your awareness of its voice. The next exercise builds on this knowledge.

Find a room where you can have some privacy and that has two chairs. Put the chairs about two feet apart, facing one another. You are going to shuttle back and forth between these two chairs. One of the chairs will represent your self-hate. The other chair will represent the part of you that is the object or target of your self-hate. Pick a side to start from and make a statement from this side. For instance, if you start with your self-hate, you might open with a statement like "I can't stand how you don't stand up for yourself with your boss. You are always letting him walk all over you. You're never going to get his respect when you act like a wimp. Grow up!" Now move to the other side and respond. The other side might say something like "I don't speak up because I am afraid of losing my job. If I listened to you, I would never be able to keep a job." Now change back to your self-hate and keep the dialogue going. Self-hate might respond and say something like "You are always afraid. It's just another excuse for you not to stand up for yourself. I am tired of all your excuses." A response to this might be something like "I am tired of trying to argue with you. You are never going to be satisfied no matter what I do or the reason I have for doing it. So I am going to stop explaining to you why I am doing what I am doing. I will listen to what you have to say to see if there is some value to it, but I am finished with accepting uncritically everything you have to say about what is going on."

You can see in this artificial dialogue that the imaginary person has begun the process of dethroning self-hate. The solution is to take the power away from your self-hate and still remain open to any valuable input from that side of you. You don't want to throw the baby out with the bathwater. The authority that you have given your self-hate must be removed if you are ever going to reconcile with yourself. This is not the same as saying that this side of you no longer serves a purpose in your life, because it does and always will. So dethrone your self-hate but don't exile it.

Some of you may be scratching your heads and saying, "How does my self-hate serve a purpose?" The answer lies in the fact that our false self is woven with our true self. The part of you that is striving to be better is also represented in your self-hate. So some of what your self-hate is communicating has value in it.

To get the most out of this exercise, try to avoid asking questions such as "Why don't you get off my back?" Instead make statements such as "Get off my back." Questions do not move the conversation along. They hide how you are really feeling, so stop hiding and start saying what you want to say. If you don't know what to say, say that. Declare whatever comes up for you at the moment. For instance, a person who has just been in the chair that represents self-hate moves to the other chair and says, "I don't know what to say to you now. I feel at a loss for words." If this is how you feel, stay with it. Stay present with your feelings and see what happens. Experiencing your impasse may create an implosion that will erupt into a mobilization of your energy and create a transformation.

Another useful tool that I teach my patients is to have them exaggerate whatever is happening. For instance, if there is no response forthcoming to one's self-hate, then it may be relevant to exaggerate the non-response. Saying something like "I will never respond to you. I am not going to waste my time dealing with you. It's better to say nothing to you than to give you credence or the opportunity to knock me down again." This declaration may help illuminate what your silence is really saying. The idea that silence means we are not communicating is a myth. We are always communicating with ourselves and others. The truth is that sometimes we don't know what our behavior is saying. We don't know how to translate some of our behavior because we don't know the key to the code. You can break your code by giving yourself permission to exaggerate and be outrageous during these exercises.

Another option to help you understand what is going on inside you is to make some sounds. Use sounds instead of words to communicate. Grunt, growl, or express whatever sound comes up for you, and go with whatever noise is there. This can help you get in touch with where you are at. The goal of this exercise is to help you become aware of your self-hate and how it manifests itself in your life. Pay close attention to your internal experiences because these cues can help you become aware of how you are feeling when your self-hate is pummeling you.

Tell your self-hate to knock it off. Inform that side of you that you will no longer buy into its absurd expectations and harsh criticisms. Tell it that you may have made mistakes but that you are not a mistake. Shout "Get off my back and leave me alone!" Declare that "I am no longer giving you the power to criticize me or control my life. Your reign is over."

Remember, the goal of this step is to block and challenge your self-hate. *It is imperative to your recovery that you get on your side and get off your back.* In order to support yourself, you need to challenge and block your self-hate. Once you have mastered this step and you can stop your self-hate, then you can replace your self-hate with self-compassion. The next step is to develop a compassionate attitude toward yourself.

When a person has difficulty with this final step, I offer the following advice: treat yourself like you would a child or close friend. We often are much more compassionate with a child or close friend than we are with ourselves. The other day I met with a woman who was in a terrible amount of emotional pain; she couldn't stand herself because of her physical illness. She suffered from a rare intestinal disease that required a colostomy bag for its treatment. She hated to wear the bag, which collected her fecal matter. She was ashamed and embarrassed. She hated herself for having this medical problem and was ashamed at the results of the intervention. I helped increase her awareness of how strongly she hated and rejected herself. Once she could spot this subterfuge beginning, I helped her learn how to block it. She responded well. During one of our sessions, while she was using the chair exercise, she was able to respond compassionately to the part of herself that was suffering from this medical condition. I asked her to imagine that she was talking to a little girl who was struggling with a similar problem. This opened up a flood of helpful and compassionate feelings, thoughts, and ideas, and she was well on her way to developing a new relationship with herself. Her first comment was "This wasn't your fault." And then she started to cry.

Life is difficult. When we experience a disappointment or failure, it is best to respond with an "of course" attitude. This can be extremely helpful and may take some of the sting out of the experience. Here are some examples:

- Of course I am having difficulty in my relationship with my wife. I am still learning how to stay centered regardless of her feelings. I need to remind myself that it is not my responsibility to satisfy her every whim.
- Of course I didn't win that tennis match. I am not used to playing against someone of that skill. I will eventually benefit from stepping up my level of competition and playing these kind of matches.
- Of course I didn't finish that project in time. I overestimated my ability to handle that project and the other requirements of my job. I will learn to be more realistic and respect my limitations.
- Of course I am having trouble writing the Fourth Step. This is a very painful experience, and I am having trouble facing many of the things about myself that I don't like. I will be more compassionate with myself as I take this Step.

This may seem like a gimmick—and it is. This gimmick is designed to help us develop a healthier perspective. Life is difficult. This is the baseline that we face yet want to deny. When we accept that life is difficult, then whatever happens is okay because the difficulty is a fact. Of course I am having trouble—life is difficult.

It also helps to keep in mind that we are not perfect. We are imperfectly human or a perfectly imperfect human. While we can strive for progress in our life, in order to find true emotional sobriety, we must surrender our special status and replace it with a spirit of acceptance and compassion while embracing the true condition of being human.

I am not offering a cop-out from trying to become a better person. I am offering a perspective that can facilitate emotional maturity by helping us learn from our mistakes. Alcoholics and addicts have trouble learning from their experience, and I believe that self-hate is the culprit. Self-hate blocks us from learning from our experiences because we are too busy beating ourselves up rather than digging into the truth.

I sincerely hope that this book has been helpful and that you have discovered some useful information and helpful perspectives. I encourage you to stay the course. Remember, life is difficult. This is the baseline. Recovery makes life even more difficult. In recovery, you are dealing with all of the givens of the human condition as well as the many challenges you encounter as you trudge the road of recovery and put your life back together. So give yourself a break, block your self-hate, and learn how to be compassionate with yourself and others. Get help if you are having trouble with any of the self-defeating behaviors I have discussed. *Get off your back and learn how to be on your side. There is hope. A miracle is always waiting for you just around the corner.*

Bibliography

Alcoholics Anonymous. 4th ed. New York: Alcoholics Anonymous World Services, 2001.

Berger, A. *How to Get the Most Out of Group Therapy.* Rev. ed. Center City, MN: Hazelden, 2007.

———. *The Therapeutic Value of the 12 Steps.* Pamphlet available at www.abphd.com.

Berger, A., with M. Palmer. *Love Secrets Revealed: What Happy Couples Know about Having Great Sex, Deep Intimacy, and a Lasting Connection.* Deerfield Beach, FL: Health Communications, 2006.

Fromm, E. *The Anatomy of Human Destructiveness.* New York: Holt, Rinehart and Winston, 1973.

Horney, K. *Neurosis and Human Growth: The Struggle toward Self-Realization.* New York: Norton, 1950.

Larsen, E. *Stage II Recovery: Life Beyond Addiction.* Minneapolis, MN: Winston Press, 1985.

London, E. D., N. G. Cascella, D. F. Wong, R. L. Phillips, R. F. Dannals, J. M. Links, R. Herning, R. Grayson, J. H. Jaffe, and H. N. Wagner Jr. "Cocaine-Induced Reduction of Glucose Utilization in Human Brain: A Study Using Positron Emission Tomography and [Fluorine 18]-Fluorodeoxyglucose." *Archives of General Psychiatry* 47, no. 6 (June 1990): 567–74.

Rubin, T. I. *Compassion and Self-Hate: An Alternative to Despair.* New York: D. McKay Co., 1975.

Schnarch, D. *Passionate Marriage: Love, Sex, and Intimacy in Emotionally Committed Relationships.* New York: W. W. Norton, 1997.

Tiebout, H. *Harry Tiebout: The Collected Writings.* Center City, MN: Hazelden, 1999.

About the Author

Allen Berger, Ph.D., is in private practice. He is also the author of *Love Secrets Revealed,* a book about making relationships work. For the past thirty-six years, Dr. Berger has been on his own personal journey in recovery while helping thousands of men and women discover a new way of life, free from addiction and its insanity. You can learn more about Dr. Berger and his work at www.abphd.com.

About Hazelden Publishing

As part of the Hazelden Betty Ford Foundation, Hazelden Publishing offers both cutting-edge educational resources and inspirational books. Our print and digital works help guide individuals in treatment and recovery, and their loved ones. Professionals who work to prevent and treat addiction also turn to Hazelden Publishing for evidence-based curricula, digital content solutions, and videos for use in schools, treatment programs, correctional programs, and electronic health records systems. We also offer training for implementation of our curricula.

Through published and digital works, Hazelden Publishing extends the reach of healing and hope to individuals, families, and communities affected by addiction and related issues.

For more information about Hazelden publications,
please call **800-328-9000**

or visit us online at **hazelden.org/bookstore**.

Other Hazelden Publishing titles that may interest you:

12 Smart Things to Do When the Booze and Drugs are Gone

Choosing Emotional Sobriety through Self-Awareness and Right Action

Allen Berger, Ph.D.

Allen Berger offers a fresh list of "smart things" to do to attain and sustain emotional sobriety. These smart things include understanding who you are and what's important to you, learning not to take others' reactions personally, trusting your inner compass, and taking responsibility for your reactions to problematic situations. It is in these practices that we find release from what Bill W. described "absolute dependency" on people or circumstances, and develop the tools to develop prestige, security, and belonging within. Softcover, 192 pp.

Order No. 2864

12 Hidden Rewards of Making Amends

Finding Forgiveness and Self-Respect by Working Steps 8-10

Allen Berger, Ph.D.

Popular author and lecturer Allen Berger, Ph.D., shares more profound recovery insights in this book, motivating us to earn the rewards that come with being honest and vulnerable. One of the many hidden rewards of working Steps Eight, Nine, and Ten is to stay in close contact with our experience so we can learn from it. *12 Hidden Rewards of Making Amends* leads to better self-understanding, which is at the heart of self-forgiveness and emotional recovery. Softcover, 232 pp.

Order No. 3968

I Want My Life Back

Steve Hamilton, with Alison Lowry

A hardened addict in his teens, the author endured eleven stays at institutions before he took his first earnest steps toward recovery. Readers will grapple with a mix of emotions as they make their way through this gritty but graceful memoir. Softcover, 392 pp.

Order No. 2146